To:
_____

REV. RAY PROBASCO, JR.

8-31-98

The Mystery
of
the Manchild

An Exposition of Revelation 12:5

The Mystery
of
the Manchild

An Exposition of Revelation 12:5

by
Willard E. Thomas
Drennon D. Stringer Jr.

DORRANCE PUBLISHING CO., INC.
PITTSBURGH, PENNSYLVANIA 15222

Dedication

I wish to dedicate this book to my loving, caring,
understanding wife, without whose Christian qualities
I could not have *endured to the end* of this book.

Willard E. Thomas

I dedicate this work to Martha, my wife, without
whose prayers, patience, support, and love this work
would never have succeeded to this distance.

Drennon D. Stringer, Jr.

Contents

FOREWORD

Reading *The Mystery of the Manchild* has fulfilled a need in my life that has been there for many years. I have always had this great fascination for the climax of history. Things eschatological have always held a high priority in my life. So when I look back to my earliest years as a believer in the Lordship of Jesus Christ, I remember that even in those early years I was fascinated by what was then called the prophetic literature surrounding *the last days.*

I can remember reading as early as the forties, and perhaps even earlier than that, about the Antichrist figures that were appearing even then in history. Some of the bolder, less careful writers were pinpointing Antichrist figures by name and prophesying that they indeed should become *the* Antichrist, the Man of Sin.

Time and history have proven most of those writers to be wrong when they attempted to name names and set dates. So early on I learned that to work in the field of eschatology one must be wise and prudent, and above all things *careful.* Once your predictions for future events are put into print, then one must live with it after those predictions have become antiquated and proven to be far from truth.

Still, the fascination of the events of *the last days* stayed with me. Always I was a believer in the Second Advent, always trying to live every day as though *that* day might be the last day before our Lord's return. I remained a steadfast student of the prophetic literature of the Scriptures.

All of that has deepened my relationship with the Savior. All of that study and that prayerful anticipation of future events have stayed with me to deepen and enrich my life. So, *Perhaps today!* has been a kind of motto for me. I have always wanted to go through life standing on tiptoes, looking eagerly for the signs of our Lord's coming again and His appearing.

Now I have discovered *The Mystery of the Manchild* and it has spoken to my mind and to my heart. It has touched me at some of the deepest recesses of my being. It has awakened for me a desire to *know Him, and the power of His resurrection, and the fellowship of His sufferings, that indeed I might be conformable unto His death.*

Willard Thomas and Drennon Stringer, dear friends of mine, have joined together for a presentation that probably has not been found in any previous literature of the last book of the Bible. They have taken the Revelation of Saint John and focused in on the twelfth chapter, and that mystifying word about the Manchild. They are attempting to answer, *Who is he?, When shall he appear?, Dare we name the name?,* and they have dealt with all of this with skill and verve, and with deep spiritual insight and a faithful reading of the Holy Scripture.

One does not have to agree with them in entirety to be blessed and to profit from their writing. One does not have to buy in to all of their interpretations of *the last days* to be edified by their writing in this seminal book. Let me commend it to you. Let me urge you to study it carefully with the Scripture open on one page and this book open along side it.

Then something beautiful will begin to happen within your soul, I devoutly believe; something deeply moving, with the Spirit of Christ touching you. This shall begin to unfold in your life in a strange and beautiful and deeply supernal way. I commend all of this to you and pray only that Christ Himself shall be honored and glorified by the dissemination of this fascinating study. We trust that it shall have a powerful and wide reading.

Dr. C. Philip Hinerman

INTRODUCTION

In 1987, the book *Cultural Literacy*[1] became a national best seller. Its subtitle intrigued many: *What Every American Needs to Know*. The author, E. D. Hirsch Jr., is a tenured English professor at the University of Virginia, well qualified to pontificate on the state of literacy in America. *Cultural Literacy* contends that America is now in a special state of *illiteracy*. Hirsch insists that American audiences lack an understanding of even the most basic assumptions of our culture. For example, a report appeared in the popular press, titled *What Do Our 17-Year-Olds Know?*[2] Using a test administered to nearly eight thousand American eleventh graders, students were tested in history and literature. The results showed that most students had no sense of when particular important historical events occurred, such as the date of the discovery of the New World. Hirsch claims that while writers, speakers, preachers, and teachers do not elaborate upon this basic knowledge of our culture, their messages presuppose an understanding of these facts. Effective communication cannot take place without a prior understanding of the most basic facts of our culture. In order

---

1. E. D. Hirsch Jr., *Cutural Literacy: What Every American Needs to Know* (Boston: Houghton Mifflin Company, 1987).
2. Diane Ravitch and Chester E. Finn Jr., *What Do Our 17-Year-Olds Know?*

for communication to be effective, Hirsch asserts, audiences must possess a certain basic level of the knowledge of the culture in which they live.

For example, suppose we wanted to deliver a message extolling the virtues of the radical concept that God became man to be offered up as the one pure sacrifice for our sins. We could employ a metaphor showing the profound significance of that act by comparing it to the discovery of the New World. We could simply say that while the discovery of the New World significantly altered the course of human existence, God's incarnation was exponentially greater. If the audience did not understand the implications of the discovery of the New World, the metaphor would be lost in a web of confusion. This critical absence of a common intellectual denominator—which Hirsch argues ought to be firmly embedded in the minds of Americans through the agency of our educational systems—is the origin of a crisis Hirsch is calling *cultural illiteracy*.

Cultural illiteracy is the insufficient grasp of elemental knowledge necessary for the intellectual health of a nation, but *cultural illiteracy* is more than that. It is a failure of communication. Ineffective communication signals the cessation of the lively exchange of ideas that created the vast richness of our American society. Because of the state of *cultural illiteracy* in America, Hirsch insists, there has been a reduction in the exchange of ideas vital to a growing and thriving populous. His thesis, then, as a professor of higher education, is that American education is failing to impart to its students our common culture necessary for a vibrant national health, a thesis confirmed by a plethora of other reports like that of Ravitch and Finn.

At this point, it may appear that this work is simply a critique of the secular mind. Let us assure you that it is not. A few years earlier, George Barna and William McKay of the American Resource Institute in Wheaton, Illinois, published their findings on the health of American Christianity. The title of their book is, *Vital Signs: Emerging Social Trends and the Future of American Christianity*.[3] Barna and

---

3. George Barna, William McKay, *Vital Signs* (Westchester: Crossway Books, 1984).

McKay conducted national public opinion surveys and behavioral research studies on a segment of our society that professed to be *born again Christians*.[4] After examining like a physician the body of believers we loosely call *the Church,* Barna and McKay concluded that Christianity's "capacity to affect society will be severely challenged."[5] They concluded that "Christians are not sufficiently armed for the struggle"[6] to socialize "*Homo sapiens* into the dominant values of the Judeo-Christian tradition, in order that they may become instruments for the transformation of our society into the kinds of eschatological utopia that God willed from the beginning of time."[7] Christianity's *coup de grace*, however, was Barna and McKay's conclusion that "any impact Christianity is having on American culture is largely happening by God's grace—in spite of His people, not because of them."[8]

What Barna and McKay discovered was that the average *born again, evangelical Christian* spends an hour a week in prayer and Bible study, but twenty-one hours watching television.[9] Twenty-five percent of *born again, evangelical Christians* who have cable television subscribe to the x-rated channels. They found that more *born again, evangelical Christian* women watch afternoon soap operas than do their non-Christian counterparts. They found that two out of three

---

4. In their surveys, Barna and McKay used the following definition of a born again Christian: someone who: 1) believes in God; 2) has made a personal commitment to Jesus Christ that is still important in their life; 3) believes that he will go to heaven because Jesus died for his sins, not because of his own merit or any works he has performed during his lifetime. *Vital Signs,* © 1984, p. 149. Used by permission of Good News Publishers/Crossway Books, 1300 Crescent Street, Wheaton, IL, 60187.
5. Ibid, p.3.
6. Ibid, p.3.
7. Tony Campolo, *You Can Make a Difference* (Dallas: Word, Inc., © 1984), p. 51, quoting his wife, Peggy Campolo. Used by permission.
8. *Vital Signs,* p.5
9. The findings of Barna and McKay are discussed throughout their book. This is merely a compilation of a few considered pertinent findings to this work here. For a deeper appreciation of their work, reading their 155-page book is recommended.

born again, evangelical Christians evidence such a great love for material things that it consumes most of their energy in the pursuit of it. Finally, they found that seven out of ten *born again, evangelical Christians* are prone to a hedonistic lifestyle, which is a way of life that puts pleasure as the highest good we can achieve. And other purveyors of Christianity had already told us that fifty percent of the *born again, evangelical Christian* population engages in premarital sex!

So while Hirsch's book sets forth the proposition that education in America is falling short of its requirement to impart our common culture to our children, studies like those done by Barna and McKay obliquely confront us to answer the question, *What is going on in the Body of Christ?* Like Hirsch's hypothesis—that there is a reduction in the transmission and exchange of thoughts and opinions vital to a growing and thriving populous—there also is a concomitant reduction in biblical literacy among *born again, evangelical Christians.* Christian men, women, and children are deplorably ignorant of the basic precepts contained in the Holy Scriptures. Like Hirsch's hypothesis—that in order for communication to be effective, readers and listeners must possess a certain level of knowledge of the culture in which they live—a similar truth applies to Christianity. Those who desire to live eternally in the presence of God also must possess a certain level of knowledge of the truths contained in the Bible. The Bible is *by necessity* the rule of faith and practice for those who want to be Christian.

The *effective* difference between Hirsch's secular hypothesis and the Christian component in this work is a religious iconoclasm: beliefs based on error must be surrendered in the face of the truth of Scripture if there is to be any hope or expectation of gaining eternal life. The *teleological*[10] difference, however, between Hirsch's secular hypothesis and the obvious Christian element in this writing, is that the consequences of biblical illiteracy are incalculably devastating: If I am but ignorant of the secular body of knowledge required to communicate effectively with my peers on an intellectual level, I will but suffer

---

10. That body of information duly subsumed under the rubric *teleology* is a specialized field within the discipline of philosophy. Simply stated, it concerns itself with the question, *What is the end result or product?* Here, it means to deal with the final state of the faithful believer of Christ.

a lifetime of rich but missed opportunities. If I am ignorant of the body of knowledge of salvation contained in the Old and New Testaments, I am liable to suffer an *eternal destruction and exclusion from the presence of the Lord, and from the glory of his might* (2 Thessalonians 1:9, RSV).

In what follows, then, is a critical re-examination of certain passages of Scripture dealing with the final state of the obedient Christian. This reinspection will no doubt challenge you to reconsider what you have already learned. It also will provide you with a unique *interpretive* perspective on Scripture. This perspective will then dispense a curious glimpse into the meaning of life. It will provide you with an uncommon insight into the mystery of our existence upon the face of this earth.

This work will also render an admonition. Jesus said, *Not every one who says to me, "Lord, Lord," shall enter the Kingdom of heaven, but he who does the will of my father who is in heaven* (Matthew 7:21, RSV). Simply mimicking those acts typically associated with living the Spirit-filled Christian life does not confirm one's position in eternal life. Indeed, the Scriptures tell us that the *Lord Jesus [will be] revealed from heaven with his mighty angels in flaming fire, inflicting vengeance upon those who do not know God and upon those who do not obey the gospel of our Lord Jesus* (2 Thessalonians 1:7-8, RSV). It therefore becomes obligatory to discover the will of God *and do it,* if we are to be counted among *the elect. This* issue will become in what follows the touchstone that separates the wheat from the tares.

It also will possess the collateral effect of defending what has been called in theological circles, *the doctrine of perseverance.*[11] But to justify the doctrine of perseverance requires that its complement, *the doctrine*

---

11. The doctrine of perseverance holds that so long as a Christian remains faithful to the end, he shall be saved from the wrath of God. The issue becomes: *What does it mean to remain faithful to the end?* The doctrine of perseverance holds that it is possible to lose the assurance of salvation by becoming unfaithful to God. Being unfaithful to God is not doing what He commands; i.e., not doing the will of God. Not doing the will of God is, in essence, living in a state of sin.

of eternal security,[12] be shunned.

Since reading the classic work of Professor Robert Shank, titled *Life in the Son,*[13] we have read no other work that so convincingly disarms and discredits the doctrine of eternal security. Both this book and the book by Professor Shank penetrate this vulnerable though popular assumption by expounding the doctrine of perseverance.

What is different in this work from that of Professor Shank's is the method of reaching the conclusion that invalidates *once saved, always saved.* Professor Shank sets out to discredit the doctrine of eternal security. So *Life in the Son* is ultimately a book refuting the assertion, *once saved, always saved.* The hypothesis in this work began, however, without any conscious regard for the doctrines of perseverance and eternal security. After twelve years of a study that produced the hypothesis contained in this work—and after standing back to behold

---

12. The doctrines of *perseverance* and *eternal security* are mutually exclusive doctrines. They cannot *both* be right. The doctrine of etemal security holds that the identity of all who shall be saved is known by God. It holds that this pre-identified group must come to the assurance of eternal salvation in Christ. It holds that if one is predestined to gain eternal life, nothing can impede the process of him doing so. A popular though erroneous interpretation of this doctrine is that once a man or woman is converted to saving faith in Christ, his lot is assured once and for all, till death him does part. Even though the *pure* form of this doctrine holds some value, it is nevertheless useless. It is useless because we will never know who makes it into heaven until we get there. The *impure* form of this doctrine holds that once a man or woman begins a new life in Christ—popularly called *being born again, accepting Christ, being converted, or getting saved*—his eternal fate is secure. It is this impure form that is refuted by the implications of the thesis contained in this work.

13. Robert Shank, *Life in the Son* (Springfield, Missouri: Westcott, 1961). It was discovered, subsequent to this writing, that *Life in the Son,* having been out of print by Westcott Publishers for a number of years, has now been republished in Minneapolis by Bethany House Publishers, 1989, in softback cover. As a critical reexamination of one of the historical tenets of theology, namely, the doctrine of perseverance, it would be well worth the time spent reading it.

the finished product—it became apparent that the hypothesis possessed a significant collateral effect. It was to refute the popular notion of *once saved, always saved,* but it came as no surprise.

Since the hypothesis contained in this work concerns itself with securing a permanent residence in eternity; and since the doctrines of eternal security and perseverance also represent issues pertaining to the same end, it was only a matter of eventually intersecting with one of these two doctrines. That point of intersection was observed *along the way,* in the process of twelve years of study. The result was an intersection with the doctrine of perseverance, and not with the doctrine of eternal security, which simply meant that the hypothesis contained herein supports the tenets of the doctrine of perseverance.

The subject matter contained in this book surrounds what previously have been unanswered questions about the future state of the believer as quixotically portrayed in the Book of the Revelation to Saint John. But—and let it be said clearly—the purpose of this book is not to frighten people into obeying the will of God. The purpose of this book is to put forth plainly the intentions of God for His people as revealed in His Word. It is an attempt to reduce the confusion emanating from biblical illiteracy about the future state of true believers. It is an attempt to get scriptural truth into the hands of a generation who very well may be the last to walk the face of earth before the return of Christ.

Like so many other literary works, however, this book is not for the many. It is for *the elect,* and for those who want to be counted among the elect. We feel a sense of urgency in getting this work into your hands, although we are timid to admit that we believe it is the prompting of the Holy Spirit to do so. We are not unduly concerned with the controversial nature of the subject matter contained herein. Instead, the sense of urgency to get this work into the hands of those who have the gift of spiritual discernment far outweighs any hope of merely contributing another theory of the end times to an already prodigious collection of the same. The time is short, we believe, before the end shall be realized. It is not a time to be bound together—by doctrine or denominational affiliation or personality leadership so common in our Christian culture—but in Christ alone.

So the hypothesis set before you, in the pages that follow, is not intended to be added to that enormous corpus of material already written about the end times. It is intended instead to tie biblical apocalyptic[14] predictions to the discussion of eternal security. It is intended to stimulate in the person who desires to be called a *true believer* a craving to seek out and obtain in his innermost being a great sense of confidence and peace when he prays, *Ever so quickly, Lord Jesus, come!*

---

14. The word *apocalypse*, from the Greek word *apokalupsis,* means *a revelation or an unveiling,* so that an apocalyptic book claims to reveal things which are normally hidden, and claims to unveil the future. Biblical apocalyptic literature proper begins with the Book of Daniel, which we will refer to, anon.

1

Who *Is* the Manchild?

And there appeared a great wonder in heaven, a woman clothed with the sun, and the moon under her feet, and upon her head a crown of twelve stars: And she being with child cried, travailing in birth, and pained to be delivered. And there appeared another wonder in heaven; and behold a great red dragon, having seven heads and ten horns, and seven crowns upon his heads. And his tail drew the third part of the stars of heaven, and did cast them to the earth: and the dragon stood before the woman which was ready to be delivered, for to devour her child as soon as it was born. And she brought forth a manchild who was to rule all nations with a rod of iron: and her child was caught up unto God, and to his throne.

—John the Revelator (Revelation 12:1-5 KJV)

Who *is* the Manchild? The mission of this book is to identify him. It is to illustrate his character. It is to catalog the implications of his design. We have searched assiduously for the meaning of the Manchild for greater than a decade. So it will not be effortless to reveal him. Early pages of this dissertation will be sprinkled heavily with scriptural references. Considerable background biblical information will be assumed in the process. However, should the reader lack a sufficient awareness of the information assumed in this work, it will not totally deny him an understanding of the hypothesis contained herein. (It is from those more familiar with Scripture that passionate objections usually arise.) If an adequate comprehension of the events recorded in the Bible is not manifest and enjoyed, reading this work will simply be an exercise of faith. It will have to be assumed that we are espousing biblical interpretations of integrity. We believe that we are. But it has been a difficult task, especially when encountering the *prophetic* or *predictive* portions of Scripture known as *apocalyptic litera-ture*. As mentioned in footnote fourteen of the Introduction, biblical apocalyptic literature proper begins and ends with the Books of Daniel and Revelation. These books are difficult to interpret. Their complexity is made obvious by the myriad volumes of interpretive and exegetical work done on them.[1] It may be, regarding the book of the Revelation to Saint John out of which comes the Manchild, that the keys to understanding its symbolic language have been obscured from most twentieth century exegetes. While this cannot be con-firmed, you can be certain of one thing regarding the understanding of God's Word:

> *And it shall come to pass in the last days, saith God, I will pour out of my Spirit upon all flesh: and your sons and your daughters shall prophesy, and your young men shall see visions, and your old men shall dream dreams: And on my servants and on my handmaidens I will pour out in those days of my Spirit; and they shall prophesy* (Acts 2:17-18, KJV).

Peter invokes this message of the Old Testament prophet Joel in his Pentecostal sermon. It is understandable that Peter believed the words of Joel spoken so many years before him were realized at Pentecost. But the verses that immediately follow, that Peter himself quotes, give circumspection to this conviction:

---

1. Some purists will argue that unless one's work has correctly grasped the meaning of the Scripture in question, the appellation *interpretation* should not be assigned to it. There is a significant element of truth in this. If we have not correctly grasped the meaning, we have not provided an inter-pretation, merely deposited *a guess*. This issue, however, becomes *How do I know when I have come to the correct understanding of a certain passage of scripture?* Many cynics disbelieve that we are still able to correctly understand the authorial intent of the biblical writers. However, we can state categorically that doing so remains an important plank in the life of God's people.

And I will shew wonders in heaven above, and signs in the earth beneath; blood, and fire, and vapour of smoke: The sun shall be turned into darkness, and the moon into blood, before that great and notable day of the Lord come: And it shall come to pass, that whosoever shall call on the name of the Lord shall be saved (Acts 2:19-21, KJV).

Evidently these last words were not intended to describe Pentecost, but another period *in the great travailing characterizing the end times.* Jesus applies this prophecy to His own Second Coming. He said:

But in those days, after that tribulation, the sun will be darkened, and the moon will not give its light, and the stars will be falling from heaven, and the powers in the heavens will be shaken. And then they will see the son of man coming in clouds with great power and glory (Mark 13:24-26 RSV).

While the scope of this book does not include an exposition of Pentecostal prophesying, it *is* about end times prophesy. Therefore, a good question to ask now is, *Are these the last days when new pieces of the apocalyptic puzzle are being revealed?* If it is, it will be a gesture signaling the imminent return of Christ. Dave Hunt is the quintessential excoriator of modern day proponents of biblical heresy, outside *and* inside the church. He writes in the opening paragraph of his latest book that,

"Somewhere, at this very moment, on planet Earth, the Antichrist is almost certainly alive—biding his time, awaiting his cue. Banal sensationalism? Far from it! That likelihood is based upon a sober evaluation of current events in relation to Bible prophecy."[2]

---

2. Taken from *Global Peace and the Rise of Antichrist* by Dave Hunt, p. 5. ©1990 by Harvest House Publishers, Eugene, Oregon, 97402. Used by permission.

Rick Joyner, a less recognized prophet of our time, wrote an article titled, *A Vision of the Harvest*. In it he considers the increased prophetic pronouncements that will accompany the closing of this age. He writes:

"The Lord will soon open our understanding of His word and purpose to a depth beyond our present comprehension. The 'books' are yet to be 'opened' as they will be. When they are and our understanding of even the basic truths such as salvation, being born again, etc. will be enormously increased [sic]. This will give far more substance and depth of purpose to the entire Body of Christ. The functions of the gifts and ministries will come with increasing authority and power as their confidence increases with knowledge." [3]

The idea of increased prophetic power, insight, and knowledge accompanying the conclusion of this age is not a novel idea. The Holy Scriptures predict the same. They declare that as the Second Coming of Christ draws near, heretofore difficult biblical prophecies will be increasingly understood. Passages that have previously been poorly understood will become transparent. Pontificating on the eventual tribulation that will characterize the closing of this age, the prophet Jeremiah says,

The fierce anger of the Lord will not turn back until he has executed and accomplished the intents of his mind. In the latter days you will understand this (Jeremiah 30:24, RSV).

The Book of Daniel also reveals that it is God's design to withhold knowledge about the end, *until* the time of the end, during the period known as *the tribulation:*

At that time shall arise Michael, the great prince who has charge of your people. And there shall be a time of trouble, such as never has been since there was a nation till that time; but at that time your people shall be delivered, every one whose name shall be found

---

3. Rick Joyner, *A Vision of the Harvest,* undated circulation, p.14. Morning Star Publications, Charlotte, North Carolina. Used by permission.

written in the book. And many of those who sleep in the dust of the earth shall awake, some to everlasting life, and some to shame and everlasting contempt. And those who are wise shall shine like the brightness of the firmament; and those who turn many to righteousness, like the stars for ever and ever. But you, Daniel, shut up the words, and seal the book, until the time of the end. [Then m]any shall run to and fro, and knowledge shall increase. Go your way, Daniel, for the words are shut up and sealed until the time of the end (Daniel 12:1-4,9, RSV).

Every generation has had its apocalyptic Cassandra who has claimed that the end was due in her lifetime. It is reasonable to assume that during the reign of one of these Cassandras the end will surely come. Not necessarily because one Cassandra was more biblical in her understanding than another, but because in every generation there has always been one who has claimed that the end is near. As Christians, we know that the end will come *eventually*. Consequently, the end must come in *someone's* generation.

"Now when these things begin to take place, look up and raise your heads, because your redemption is drawing near." And he told them a parable: "Look at the fig tree, and all the trees; as soon as they come out in leaf, you see for yourselves and know that the summer is already near. So also, when you see these things taking place, you know that the kingdom of God is near. Truly, I say to you, this generation will not pass away till all has taken place" (Luke 21:28-32, RSV).

While the Scriptures implore us not to pinpoint dates, it is nevertheless reasonable and prudent to conclude with even a cursory reading of those sections of the Bible that deal with the subject matter of the end times, that we are definitely in the beginning of the end. While we will not proclaim that we are mouthpieces to be used by God in the end times, we will convey what we understand about the meanings of certain biblical passages as they apply to this mysterious figure called the Manchild. The Manchild *is* very much tied to the subject matter dealing with the predictions of the end of the world.

So the appropriate place to begin an investigation of the Manchild would be the text quoted at the beginning of this chapter, namely, Revelation 12:1-5. Looking at this text, it becomes necessary to ask and answer a series of questions made obvious by it. *Who is the woman? Who is the dragon?* And finally, *Who is the Manchild?*

Who Is the Woman?

Expositors generally agree that the woman in Revelation 12 represents the nation of Israel. There are, however, many explanations that have been offered in the just as many commentaries.[4] Let us not so quickly join in agreement upon this simply because conventional scholarly wisdom so dictates. Let us examine the evidence first hand to see if a justification of integrity can be found.

In the first verse of the twelfth chapter of Revelation the woman is in heaven. In verse two the woman is still in heaven, but now pregnant. Verse four depicts the dragon standing before the woman travailing in birth. By verse five, the woman has delivered the Manchild, but has done so on earth. And in verse six the woman has fled into the wilderness *postpartum*. Obviously then, the woman cannot be a literal person. There is no known person in human history who existed pregnant in heaven to descend subsequently to the earth beneath to deliver her child. The woman is conspicuously a symbol representative of another meaning, a literary device not uncommon in biblical literature.

Within the realm of biblical hermeneutics (the art of biblical interpretation), *a symbol is a sign that suggests meaning, rather than stating it.*[5] So we may ask with curiosity, *What meaning is suggested by the symbolic woman?* Part of the answer lies in the crown of twelve stars upon her head. Here the usage of numbers is employed, appropriately called *biblical numerology*.

Biblical numerology is also a common literary device exploited at various places throughout Scripture. As modern-day purveyors of the Revelation to Saint John, we are disadvantaged in our capacity to

---

4. Other than the definition that follows, the second most popular explanation of the woman is that she is the Virgin Mary. This popular opinion will be dealt with in the section containing the discussion of the answer to the question, *Who is the Manchild?*
5. A. Berkeley Mickelsen, *Interpreting the Bible* (Grand Rapids: William B. Eerdmans, 1963), p. 271.

adequately understand biblical numerology. We are particularly afflicted in our capacity to understand the biblical symbolism used to represent the historic people of God. Our conversations are rarely sprinkled with the seasoning of a discussion surrounding the historic people of God. The usage of symbols like the woman with a crown of twelve stars upon her head was no doubt easily understood by the author's contemporary readers. Their dialog was intimately tied to the employment of symbolic representations. Little explanation was needed to convince John the Revelator's audience of the woman's symbolic nature. As modern-day consumers of the literature of old, a little diligent effort is required to rediscover what John intended by the symbolism of the woman.

A meager investigation discloses that the number twelve holds special significance. It is *the typical number of the unbrokenness, of the irreducible completeness of the theocratic people, of the people for God's own possession.*[6] It cannot be disputed that the nation of Israel represents God's chosen people. However, Israel is far more than a people of God's own choosing. She is *the wife of God:*

> For thy Maker is thine husband; The Lord of hosts is his name. I am married unto you (Isaiah 54:5, Jeremiah 3:14, KJV).

But the wife of God is unfaithful, a condition metaphorically portrayed in the terms of sexual reproduction. In Isaiah 26:17-18 the nation of Israel is talking to God. She says:

> Like as a woman with child, that draweth near the time of her delivery, is in pain, and crieth out in her pangs; so have we been in thy sight, O Lord. We have been with child, we have been in pain, we have as it were brought forth wind (KJV).

During the prophetic reign of Isaiah, the message of God lamented the barrenness of His wife, the nation of Israel. Isaiah mourns that she has been unable to do more than *break wind.* As the bride of

---

6. K. H. Rengstorf, *Theologisches Worteruchzum Neuen Testament.* Ed., Gerhard Kittel. Vol. II (Stuttgart: Verlag von W. Kohlhammer, 1935), p. 323.

God, Israel is expected to be fruitful and multiply, but she has not yet produced the anticipated offspring yearned for and foreordained by her husband God. In spite of the words of encouragement, Israel fails to produce the child of God's longing. Read further the words of the Prophet Isaiah:

> *Sing, O barren, thou that didst not bear; break forth into singing, and cry aloud, thou that didst not travail with child: for more are the children of the desolate than the children of the married wife, saith the Lord. Enlarge the place of thy tent, and let them stretch forth the curtains of thine habitations: spare not, lengthen thy cords, and strengthen thy stakes; for thou shall break forth on the right hand and on the left; and thy seed shall inherit the Gentiles* (Isaiah 54: 1-3, KJV).

Because the nation of Israel is backslidden and unfaithful, God prophesies through Isaiah that a time would come when He would look beyond the Jewish nation to fulfill the parturient demands of His chosen people. God's unrelenting and passionate desire to behold an offspring compels Him to employ an alternate method for obtaining the desired progeny. Isaiah 54:3 *therefore prophesies the inclusion of the Gentiles into the plan of salvation for the world.* The Prophet Micah then declares the timetable of Israel's abandonment by God:

> *But you, O Bethlehem Ephrathah, who are little to be among the clans of Judah, from you shall come forth for [God] one who is to be ruler in Israel, whose origin is from of old, from ancient days. Therefore [God] shall give them up, until the time when she who is in travail has brought forth; then the rest of [Christ's] brethren shall return to the people of Israel* (Micah 5:2-3, RSV).

The *she* referred to by the Prophet Micah is the pregnant bride of God. Scripture has again used the metaphor of human sexuality to portray divine intent. God is the husband. The nation of Israel is His wife. Together they conceive to bear a child. She is pregnant, awaiting their first child.

After scrutinizing Scripture it is apparent that the nation of Israel does not produce *a single child* until the time of Revelation 12. Until *the time of the end,* she will not deliver the anticipated offspring. The woman of Revelation 12 is the nation of Israel that has been destined by God to deliver His child. She represents a community of beings ordained with divine intent. When she who is now serving as the pregnant bride of God delivers the child within her womb, *it will be the Manchild of Revelation 12.*

So the woman of Revelation 12 is the pregnant bride of God. When she delivers, she will thus fulfill her duty as the wife of God, to produce a child out of the aching of God's own heart. Her offspring, the Manchild, will be God's long-awaited child. J. A. Seiss, commenting upon the identity of the pregnant woman in Revelation 12, remarks that,

> "this mystic woman is in the way of motherhood. Within her body, concealed from human view but consciously to herself, there is a mystic seed, maturing for manifestation, to bring which to the birth is the one great object of His most intense anxieties." [7]

Who is the dragon?

While there is some disagreement surrounding the identity of the symbolic woman in Revelation 12, there is practically no disagreement surrounding the personality of the dragon. The reason for this is that Revelation 12:9 renders his name.

> *And the great dragon was thrown down, that ancient serpent, who is called the devil and satan, the deceiver of the whole world* (RSV).

Not much needs to be said about John's usage of the symbolic dragon. What can be said, however, is that there is a consistency in John's literary device. That is, *the woman* is a symbol suggesting meaning, and *the dragon* is a symbol suggesting meaning. *The woman* and *the dragon* are representatives of the nation of Israel and the devil,

---

7. J. A. Seiss, *A Zondervan Commentary: The Apocalypse: Lectures on the Book of Revelation* (Elgin, Illinois: Charles C. Cook, 1900), p. 296. (Although publishing laws state that material published in 1900 is now under public domain, if you are aware of any renewed copyright claims upon this work, please contact us and additional reprints will include acknowledgment.)

respectively.[8] Each also represents a community of beings. *The woman* represents the people of God. And *the dragon* represents Satan and his *aides-de-camp*. Revelation 12:4 declares that when Satan fell from heaven, he took with him a *third of the stars of heaven*. Conventional scholarly wisdom decrees that *a third of the stars of heaven* means that he took with him from heaven at the time of his fall a third of the heavenly hosts of angels. As will be shown below, it is imperative that the symbolic Manchild also represents a community of beings as well. Let us now turn to the third symbol employed by John the Revelator, namely, *the Manchild*.

Who is the Manchild?

There are considerable differences of opinions surrounding the identity of the Manchild. Who—or what—is the Manchild? It is around the interpretation of this symbolic figure that exists quite a bit of confusion among learned men. Because the Manchild is mentioned in such close proximity (in the same pericope) with the other symbols (the woman and the dragon), it must be assumed that the Manchild is also a symbol suggesting meaning. Furthermore, since the woman and the dragon each represent a community of beings, the Manchild also must represent a community of beings as well. Many commentaries acknowledge the symbolic natures of the woman and the dragon.

---

8. It was mentioned earlier that John's contemporary audience possessed an advantage for assessing the meaning of the woman in Revelation 12. While the symbolic nature of the woman was no doubt easily understood by those early Christians who were familiar with its usage, the symbolic usage of *the dragon* was not. Biblical traditions with their symbolic representations of the nation of Israel were well known to those early readers of the material we now call the Book of the Revelation to Saint John. But John the Revelator was forging uncharted territory, namely, apocalyptic revelation. Therefore, it was required of him to provide an accompanying explanation for the symbolic dragon. The symbolic usage of the dragon was not easily understood by his contemporary audience. They were unfamiliar with its meaning. So John apparently took the time to define *the dragon* in the text. His doing so therefore makes it easily understood by modern, twentieth century audiences.

Then they sense the need to employ another literary device called *literalism* when attempting to catalog the identity of the Manchild. That is, while acknowledging that *the woman* and *the dragon* are symbols, a plethora of commentaries nevertheless switches gears by claiming that the Manchild is literally Jesus. This seems, however, to be mixing metaphors—to acknowledge that a literal Jesus in the actual person of the Manchild is being born of a symbolic woman representing the nation of Israel, standing before a symbolic beast representing the devil. *Why then can't the Manchild literally be Jesus, and the woman literally be the Virgin Mary?*

In reading the profusion of explanations available surrounding the identity of the Manchild, it seems that so many have properly understood a good many fragments of the overall and difficult apocalyptic puzzle contained in the Revelation to Saint John. Sufficient credit is due them for their great work, but—and this is not intended to be critical, because the corpus of material we are dealing with is extremely difficult and mind boggling—many commentaries are like the obsessive parochial artist interested in a single color of his infatuation. When he views the beauty of the mosaic made of small pieces of colored glass inlaid to form the design of artistic value, he notices only the color of his obsession, and not at all the other wonderfully colored pieces of glass so important to the work of art *in toto*. His color of obsession no doubt adds to the beauty of the piece, but is by no means the celebrated element. So, too, have bits and pieces been celebrated in the commentaries that are attempting to explain the segments of the apocalyptic puzzle containing the celebrated Manchild.

So what about the possibility of the Manchild being Jesus, and the woman being the Virgin Mary?

Most have claimed, in one form or another, that the Manchild is Christ Himself, and that the verses mentioning the Manchild must therefore refer to His birth out of the womb of the Virgin Mary. While we appreciate the attempt to explain rationally the multifarious Book of the Revelation to Saint John, we must nevertheless reject all attempts to define the Manchild as solely Christ Himself.[9] We have

---

9. We do believe, as will be shown later, that Christ is definitely *part of* the constitution of the Manchild.

already established that the woman is no known human representative, that she is a symbol of the nation of Israel. How then could she be the Virgin Mary? The more forceful argument for the dismissal of these explanations as erroneous, however, is that the attempt to equate the Manchild with Christ Himself does not consider that *the birth* of the Manchild comes during the blowing of the seventh trumpet of Revelation. We need only look to Christ's own great prophetic discourse on the end times to see what He says is associated with the blowing of the last trumpet.

> *Immediately after the tribulation of those days the sun will be darkened, and the moon will not give its light, and the stars will fall from heaven, and the powers of the heavens will be shaken; then will appear the sign of the Son of man in heaven, and then all the tribes of the earth will mourn, and they will see the Son of man coming on the clouds of heaven with power and great glory; and he will send out his angels with a loud trumpet call, and they will gather his elect from the four winds, from one end of heaven to the other* (Matthew 24:29-31, RSV).

And in 1 Corinthians 15:51-52 Paul says:

> *Lo! I tell you a mystery. We shall not all sleep, but we shall be changed, in a moment, in the twinkling of an eye, at the last trumpet. For the trumpet will sound, and the dead will be raised imperishable, and we shall be changed* (RSV).

The subject of the last and seventh blowing trumpet is Christ's coming, and the concomitant end of the world. It is therefore insurmountable to reckon the biblical chronology of the Manchild being born *at sometime in the future* under the seventh trumpet, with the anachronistic birth of Jesus out of the womb of Mary *nearly two thousands years ago.*

J. A. Seiss was quoted earlier in this work, and once again his name and work on the Book of the Revelation to Saint John is invoked. Seiss was born greater than a sesquicentennial ago. His thesis on the constitution of the Manchild sheds considerable light upon his identity. He is quoted at length below on his dissertation of Revelation 12 for two reasons: one, because of his antiquity; and two, because of the clarity with which he writes concerning the Manchild so many years before us.

> "Still another landmark in the case [of discerning the identity of the Manchild] is that the birth here spoken of is not consummated before the period of the end of this age. Whatever earnests of it may have preceded, it is not fully accomplished till the day of judgment comes. It is here placed under the seventh trumpet, and the seventh trumpet is the last, with which the whole history of this present world ends. Accordingly, this child is unborn until the period of the end is reached. We cannot, therefore, legitimately understand it of anything in the history of the Church [including the birth of Christ to the Virgin Mary], or of anything that comes to its maturity and is outwardly manifested, anterior to the judgment times. This one particular in the presentation, so clear and conspicuous that we dare by no means ignore it, of itself utterly sweeps away four-fifths of all the commentation on the subject as irrelevant, unallowable, and only clouding the truth intended to be exhibited. Any and everything, of whatsoever kind or character, which is born, matured and outwardly manifested, prior to the day of judgment, is not, and cannot be, this man-child; for he is not born, at least his birth is not fully accomplished, till the seventh trumpet sounds, and the end of the world is come." [10]

While Rick Joyner suggests that a greater understanding of the Scriptures will accompany the beginning of the end, one might postulate that the beginning of the end began in 1823 when J. A. Seiss was born, only to write subsequently this commentary on the identity of the Manchild!

So, having cleared sufficient thistles from the apocalyptic hermeneutics, we are now able to more clearly decipher the identity of the Manchild. From Revelation 12:5 we observe that the Manchild is *to rule all the nations with a rod of iron*. He is to reign with unrivalled and irresistible authority and power over all the world. He is to govern,

---

10. J. A. Seiss, A *Zondervan Commentary: The Apocalypse: Lectures on the Book of Revelation* (Elgin, Illinois: Charles C. Cook, 1900), p. 297.

---

discipline, and control all the peoples of the earth. His dominion leaves none outside it. His rule shall be universal. The Manchild shall rule the eschatological kingdom of God. Strength, absoluteness, and perpetuity of rule are his unmistakable characteristics, that shall be exercised over *all the nations*. But the Manchild, symbolic of a company of beings, will not represent a company of supernatural individuals. The Manchild will be comprised of what were once common human beings. From the days of the ancient prophets God's divine promise has been that,

> *the kingdom and the dominion and the greatness of the kingdoms under the whole heaven shall be given to the people of the saints of the Most High; their kingdom shall be an everlasting kingdom* (Daniel 7:27, RSV).

The Manchild shall consist of *saints*. Everyone whom grace has called is called to be a joint heir and king in the future kingdom of God. Everyone redeemed by the Blood of Christ, sanctified by the Holy Spirit, and found doing the will of God will be anointed the beneficiary of eternal regency. The Manchild shall consist of saints who had endured to the end, who had remained faithful to the end, and who had accomplished the will of God during their lifetime. And since the woman of Revelation 12 is God's bride, we may rightfully desire to extend the metaphor by pondering the moment of the conception of the Manchild within her womb. Thus an examination of the Word of God reveals the answer to this question.

> *[E]ven as he chose us in Him before the foundation of the world, that we should be holy and blameless before him. He destined us in love to be his sons through Jesus Christ, according to the purpose of his will. For those whom He foreknew He also predestined to be conformed to the image of his Son, in order that He might be the first-born among many brethren* (Ephesians 1:4-5; Romans 8:29, RSV).

Notice the relationship between Micah 5:3 and Romans 8:29. Micah 5:3, Romans 8:29, *et al.,* inform us that Jesus will be the first born of the marriage between God and Israel. After *His* birth, Ephesians 1:4-5, *et al.,* inform us that we also shall be their offspring, as brothers of Christ. *Christ and His brethren are to comprise the family of God.* More than that, however, *it is Christ and His brethren that have been the long-expected offspring of God's own heart, the Manchild of Revelation 12.* God destined before the beginning of time that those whom He would create might also be *in Him.* That time of our predestination was the instant which we could consider to be the moment of the conception of the Manchild.

It does not, however, end there. God ordained that those who remain *in Him* until the end should eventually become something more than a nation of people just created in His image, existing simply to replenish the population on earth until the end of time. The Apostle Paul in his Epistle to the Ephesians declares that:

> *He has made known to us in all wisdom and insight the mystery of his will, according to his purpose which He set forth in Christ as a plan for the fullness of time, to unite all things in Him, things in heaven and things on earth* (Ephesians 1:9-10, RSV).

The unfolding of *the mystery*[11] shall be realized in *the fullness of time.* That is, it shall be consummated at *the birth* of the Manchild. The birth of the Manchild shall signal the completion of God's uniting *all things in Him.*

Paul in his Epistle to the Ephesians refers to those who are *in Christ.*[12] While the nation of Israel was intended from the beginning of time to be in Christ (and this is important), the *nation of Israel was also intended from the beginning of time to be the catalyst for producing this very important offspring.* The importance of Revelation 12 is not so much that the woman is the nation of Israel. It is that God had destined the nation of Israel to be His wife for the purpose of producing a very special child for a very special eschatological purpose. The

---

11. Chapter Three, titled, *God's Mystery of the Ages,* details this most important concept of *the mystery of God* sprinkled throughout Scripture.
12. The phrase *in Christ* represents a most significant and important qualifier. There is no doubt that those who remain *in Christ* will be saved from eternal destruction and separation from the glory of God. The pivotal issue, *What does it mean to be in Christ?*

purpose of the Manchild is the great mystery of the ages now revealed to us through the Holy Scriptures. Jesus said that,

He who conquers and who keeps my works until the end, I will give him power over the nations, and he shall rule them with a rod of iron, as when earthen pots are broken in pieces, even as I myself have received power from my Father (Revelation 2:26-27, RSV).

J. A. Seiss refers below to the Second Psalm. The Second Psalm concerns itself with *the judgment* at the end of time. To understand more effectively the quotation by Seiss, we quote Psalm 2:4-11.

He who sits in the heavens laughs; the Lord has them in derision. Then he will speak to them in his wrath, and terrify them in his furry, saying, "I have set my king on Zion, my holy hill." I will tell of the decree of the Lord. He said to me, "You are my son, today I have begotten you. Ask of me, and I will make the nations your heritage, and the ends of the earth your possession. You shall break them with a rod of iron, and dash them in pieces like a potter's vessel." Now therefore, O kings, be wise; be warned, O rulers of the earth. Serve the Lord with fear, with trembling kiss his feet, lest he be angry, and you perish in the way; for His wrath is quickly kindled. Blessed are all who take refuge in Him (RSV).

Now, the words of J. A. Seiss:

"Those who profess to find the fulfillment of [the Manchild] in the times long past, are still constrained to admit, that the language touching the official destiny of this child falls in precisely with the second Psalm. And yet that Psalm refers particularly to the judgment time, and preeminently to Jesus Christ, that greatest Son, as well as Lord, of the Church, in whom and with whom all the blessed and holy who have part in 'the first resurrection' shall 'reign' and 'judge' in a supernal and immortal administration . . . The description fits to the true saints of God of every generation, with the glorified Jesus at their head." [13]

13.J. A. Seiss, *A Zondervan Commentary: The Apocalypse: Lectures on the Book of Revelation* (Elgin, Illinois: Charles C. Cook, 1900), p. 299.

2

Old Testament Predictions
of the Manchild

This was the dream; now we will tell the king its interpretation. You, O king, the king of kings, to whom the God of heaven has given the kingdom, the power, and the might, and the glory, and into whose hand he has given, wherever they dwell, the sons of men, the beasts of the field, and the birds of the air, making you rule over them all—you are the head of gold. After you shall arise another kingdom inferior to you, and yet a third kingdom of bronze, which shall rule over all the earth. And there shall be a fourth kingdom, strong as iron, because iron breaks to pieces and shatters all things; and like iron which crushes, it shall break and crush all these. And as you saw the feet and toes partly of potter's clay and partly of iron, it shall be a divided kingdom; but some of the firmness of iron shall be in it, just as you saw iron mixed with the miry clay. And as the toes of the feet were partly iron and partly clay, so the kingdom shall be partly strong and partly brittle. As you saw the iron mixed with miry clay, so they will mix with one another in marriage, but they will not hold together, just as iron does not mix with clay.

—The Prophet Daniel (Daniel 2:36-43, RSV)

In chapter one it was suggested that the Revelation to Saint John was a very difficult book to interpret. This is made obvious by the tomes of interpretative work done on it by the various and sundry scholars down through the ages. However, if the Revelation to Saint

John is considered one of the more difficult books to interpret, the Book of Daniel, quoted in part above, might also be considered to reside in this class of books as well. The difficulty in interpreting the Book of Daniel is no doubt due in part to the fact that its style is so similar to that of the Revelation to Saint John, a similarity that lends itself to a literary intrigue that titillates the mind of the journeyman scholar who is interested in the art of hermeneutics. As a matter of fact, the subject matter of this chapter emanated from an exploration of this literary intrigue, an exploration whose fruition was the discovery of an Old Testament adumbration of the New Testament concept of the Manchild.

In general, an adumbration is that which represents something by pointing to it, by merely outlining it, or by indicating it vaguely. But specifically, in order to clarify its usage in this work, it can be said that an adumbration is intended to refer to certain portions of Scripture that point but vaguely to a concept defined in certain chronologically subsequent Scripture. When these subsequent portions of Scripture are interpreted, it is only then that we can go back to the respective (chronologically occurring) earlier portions of Scripture (if any exists) to see that these chronologically occurring earlier portions of Scripture were indeed pointing to—adumbrating—the concept in question promulgated in the subsequent Scripture. Similarly, it is only when these chronologically occurring earlier portions of Scripture are read in light of certain later Scriptures that the adumbration in them can be discovered.

The primary purpose of this chapter, then, is to establish the presence of an adumbration in the Book of Daniel that points to the concept of the Manchild found in the Revelation to Saint John. In so doing, we would like to look at two examples of parallel passages of Scripture that concern themselves with similar visions. In each case, a passage out of the Revelation to Saint John will be cited along with a passage out of the Old Testament. As we shall see, John the Revelator, under the inspiration of the Holy Spirit, was given the same visions that the Prophets Zechariah and Ezekiel were given. But more importantly, John the Revelator, under the inspiration of the Holy Spirit, was also given the same vision that King Nebuchadnezzar envisioned. To the first of these two examples, let us now turn.

The First Example, The Two Olive Trees (Zechariah 4:1-5, 11-14, RSV)

And the angel who talked with me came again, and waked me, like a man that is wakened out of his sleep. And he said to me, "What do you see?" I said, "I see, and behold, a lampstand all of gold, with a bowl on the top of it, and seven lamps on it, with seven lips on each of the lamps which are on the top of it. And there are two olive trees by it, one on the right of the bowl and the other on its left." And I said to the angel who talked with me, "What are these, my lord?" Then the angel who talked with me answered me, "Do you not know what these are?" I said, "No, my lord." Then I said to him, "What are these two olive trees on the right and the left of the lampstand?" And a second time I said to him, "What are these two branches of the olive trees, which are beside the two golden pipes from which the oil is poured out?" He said to me, "Do you not know what these are?" I said, "No, my lord." Then he said, "These are the two anointed who stand by the Lord of the whole earth."

In this passage from the Book of Zechariah we find the visional symbol of the golden candlestick with a bowl atop its base, from which seven pipes protruded to bring the necessary oil for igniting seven lamps. Beside the candlestick were two olive trees. The two olive trees were supposed to be a constant source of fuel oil for the bowls' reservoirs atop the lampstands. But the Prophet Zechariah was puzzled by his own vision. So he asked twice the accompanying angel for the meaning of the two olive trees. The angel's reply, after Zechariah's twice-repeated question, suggests that the answer should have been self-evident to Zechariah. So the angel answers in a slightly enigmatic form, saying, *These are the two anointed who stand before the Lord of the whole earth.* Zechariah's visional symbol of the two olive trees then serves as the basis for a second visional symbol for John the Revelator many years later:[1]

---

1. It is only coincidental that the subject matter of the second part of this example (that we are about to examine) is also integral to the theory of *The Mystery of the Manchild*. This example, namely, the pericope of the two witnesses who will be slain and left in the streets unburied (the Revelation to Saint John 11:3-12), will be discussed in much fuller detail in

And I will grant my two witnesses power to prophesy for one thousand two hundred and sixty days, clothed in sackcloth. These are the two olive trees and the two lampstands which stand before the Lord of the earth. And if any one would harm them, fire pours from their mouth and consumes their foes; if any one would harm them, thus he is doomed to be killed. They have power to shut the sky, that no rain may fall during the days of their prophesying, and they have power over the waters to turn them into blood, and to smite the earth with every plague, as often as they desire. And when they have finished their testimony, the beast that ascends from the bottomless pit will make war upon them and conquer them and kill them, and their dead bodies will lie in the street of the great city that is allegorically called Sodom and Egypt, where their Lord was crucified. For three days and a half men from the peoples and tribes and tongues and nations gaze at their dead bodies and refuse to let them be placed in a tomb, and those who dwell on the earth will rejoice over them and make merry and exchange presents, because these two prophets had been a torment to those who dwell on the earth. But after the three and a half days a breath of life from God entered them, and they stood up on their feet, and great fear fell on those who saw them. Then they heard a loud voice from heaven saying to them, "Come up hither!" And in the sight of their foes they went up to heaven in a cloud (The Revelation to Saint John 11:3-12, RSV).

In the Revelation to Saint John, inspired by the work of the Holy Spirit, John envisions two witnesses or prophets whose ministry extends for three-and-a-half years. He designates these two prophets as *the two olive trees and the two lampstands which stand before the Lord of the earth.* In this passage, each witness or prophet is symbolized by a lampstand and by an olive tree. By this symbolism, John no doubt intended to convey the message that the two witnesses shall be divinely empowered for their supernatural ministry. John implied that they were to be supplied with oil. This obviously means that they are to be empowered by the presence of God in their lives. Indeed, they will be like two *anointed who stand by the Lord of the whole earth* (Zechariah 4:14).

---

chapter seven, where its unique meaning and significance will be given as it specifically relates to the concept of the Manchild.

The similarities between the visions of Zechariah and John the Revelator are not just coincidental. In both cases, the vision was given by God. For those of us who believe in the supernatural inspiration of Scripture through the work of the Holy Spirit, little else needs to be said to defend the proposition that these occurrences are not just coincidental. Let us now turn to the second and last example.

The Second Example, The Eating of Scrolls

But you, son of man, hear what I say to you; be not rebellious like that rebellious house; open your mouth, and eat what I give you. And when I looked, behold, a hand was stretched out to me, and, lo, a written scroll was in it; and he spread it before me; and it had writing on the front and on the back, and there were written on it words of lamentation and mourning and woe. And he said to me, "Son of man, eat what is offered to you; eat this scroll, and go, speak to the house of Israel." So I opened my mouth, and he gave me the scroll to eat. And he said to me, "Son of man, eat this scroll that I give you and fill your stomach with it." Then I ate it; and it was in my mouth as sweet as honey. (Ezekiel 2:8-3:3, RSV).

Then I saw another mighty angel coming down from heaven. He had a little scroll open in his hand. Then the voice which I had heard from heaven spoke to me again, saying, "Go, take the scroll which is open in the hand of the angel who is standing on the sea and on the land." So I went to the angel and told him to give me the little scroll; and he said to me, "Take it and eat; it will be bitter to your stomach, but sweet as honey in your mouth." And I took the little scroll from the hand of the angel and ate it; it was sweet as honey in my mouth, but when I had eaten it my stomach was made bitter (Revelation 10:1-2, 8-11, RSV).

In these two portions of Scripture we observe what is known to students of the art of hermeneutics as *emblematic action*. Emblematic action refers to a scriptural occurrence of a prophetic action that symbolizes or suggests an idea that lives vividly in the minds of those who observe it, or in the minds of those who participate in the action. Emblematic action in Scripture is drama at its best. The actor—usually the prophet himself—not only conveys a message to himself and to others. He lives out his own life in the vision, and not the life of another. The prophet himself—along with the action he executes—becomes the symbol itself.

Ad rem, both Ezekiel and John the Revelator were commanded to take a scroll and eat it. In Ezekiel this becomes an action signifying the instituting of his call or commission. In the Revelation to Saint John the symbolic action is described in a section in which John's divinely appointed call to ministry is reaffirmed. John, through the voice of the vision, is told that his ministry as a prophet is not yet finished. The contents of the book that Ezekiel ate contained lamentations, mourning, and woe, like much of the message that he brought to his people. The book that John took and ate seems to have contained a picture of the climax of human history as we know it, in which the ruling, reigning body of Christ will be established. It is a climax in which the people of God will experience suffering and blessings unparalleled in times previous. Those who are opposed to God will know judgment and banishment from His presence. As in Ezekiel, the rest of the Revelation to Saint John (chapters 11-22) sets forth the themes covered as *the mystery*[2] of God and is brought to completion (Revelation 10:7). But the symbolic action, both for Ezekiel and for John, is focused on the act of eating the book. In the case of John, equal attention is given to the result of the digestive process. Ezekiel says that the scroll was in his mouth as honey for sweetness (Ezekiel 3:3). John is told of a twofold effect. In his mouth it will be as sweet as honey, but in the stomach it will be bitter. When John actually carried out the divine command to eat, the results were exactly as the angel had said they would be.

From this second example, it is obvious that there also are similarities between the visions of John the Revelator and Ezekiel. This, too, is not just coincidental. *John the Revelator was being inspired by the Holy Spirit to write Scripture.* John, under the inspiration of the Holy Spirit, envisioned the same visions as the Prophets Zechariah and Ezekiel.

This may be akin to the ancient aphorism of *not seeing the forest for the trees.* If our perspective of the inspiration of Holy Scripture is not

---

2. The concept of *the mystery of God* holds special importance *vis-a-vis* apocalyptic eschatology, which will be discussed in the following chapter.

high, the parallel similarities between the aforementioned examples may seem but casual. However, *God is the author of these visions.* If you are like one with a typical curiosity, the answer to the following question becomes a practical compelling necessity: *Is there a significant reason why God chose to give similar visions to John that He gave to the prophets of old?* Obviously, to this journeyman scholar, a rather high view of the inspiration of Scripture is held, such that mere coincidence or casual duplicity must be ruled out. This hypothesis is further affirmed as we examine yet another parallel occurrence of a vision from the Old Testament also experienced by John the Revelator. Under the inspiration of the Holy Spirit, John envisioned, as shall be discussed next, the same vision that King Nebuchadnezzar envisioned. We must not simply discount these three occurrences as mere coincidence. Rather, let us engage our utmost concentration in the hermeneutics of apocalyptic eschatology, for it may be that God is trying to tell us something so incredible and iconoclastic that we should sit erect and pay full attention. And if we do so, we shall behold the revealing of the mystery of the ages which answers the question of why God initially created man to replenish the earth; a *why* that goes beyond the reason to love and obey God all the days of our life.

At this point, then, we would like to turn to the presentation of the discussion of King Nebuchadnezzar's dream. This will be done by using the vehicle of detailing the epistemological[3] pathway that led to the discovery of the adumbration of the Manchild from the Revelation to Saint John in the prophetic Book of Daniel. To that, we now turn.

---

3. No equivocation is intended by the usage of the word *epistemological.* It is merely an appropriate term referring to how human beings come to know *anything.* Especially for Christians, some of our *knowing* begins through the work of the Holy Spirit. While we must exercise our own wills to do our own homework when it comes to interpreting the Scriptures, a man whose will *is to do His will, [can] know whether the teaching is from God* (John 7:17, RSV). Ultimately, that *knowing* is the result of the Holy Spirit speaking to us for the purpose of giving to us His knowledge, His truth, and His will.

The first epistemological step leading to the discovery of the adumbration of the Manchild from the Revelation to Saint John in the Book of Daniel was taken when the text quoted at the beginning of chapter one of this book, namely, Revelation 12:1-5, was read and reread, over and over, again and again. This portion of Scripture contains the first mention of the concept of the Manchild throughout the entire Bible, interestingly found in the last book of the Bible. In those early days of reading and rereading the text on the birth of the Manchild, its identity was elusive. Wanting to discover what God through the use of John the Revelator intended for journeyman Bible scholars like us to understand by its usage, we continued rereading Revelation 12:1-5 in hopes of eventually grasping its meaning. And the more we reread that text, the more we experienced a cerebral tickling (which was later ascribed to the movement of the Holy Spirit), a titillation of a faint memory of something we had read before, a titillation suggesting that we had previously encountered an adumbration of the Manchild, though we had never thought of that reading (whatever it was) in the context of an adumbration.

This early cerebral tickling produced a low level awareness of the thing to be remembered, that existed only but obliquely in memory, like the conscious but unattenuated awareness of other pedestrians on a busy downtown New York City street during an early morning rush hour; that is, each of those pedestrians possesses a unique life whose meaning could not possibly be understood unless we stopped to familiarize ourselves with each of them. Hence—extending the metaphor—we mentally stopped to become familiar with the details of the faint memory elicited by the rereading of Revelation 12:1-5 to discover that quite possibly the details of that noetic stimulation might lay in the Book of Daniel. Ascribing the metaphysics[4] of noetic

---

4. Again, no equivocation is intended by the usage of the word *metaphysics*. Like the term *epistemological, metaphysics* also refers to *knowing*. It is merely a method of inquiry employed when one attempts to consult the earliest source of knowledge. It is a science that attempts to establish a so-called *First Knowledge*. For Christians, as it was in the case for Christian epistemology, Christian metaphysics assumes that God is the very earliest

stimulation to the work of the Holy Spirit, we felt prevailed upon to return to the Book of Daniel. And it was there, in the early chapters of the Book of Daniel, that we discovered the adumbration of the Manchild found in Revelation 12:1-5.

It is in the early chapters of the Book of Daniel that we can find significant historical episodes of the life and reign of the great and powerful king of Babylon, King Nebuchadnezzar. Writing from the significant vantage point of one intimately associated with King Nebuchadnezzar, Daniel chronicles a unique historical account in chapter two. Chapter two in the Book of Daniel concerns itself with a certain nocturnal dream which troubled King Nebuchadnezzar one night. Knowing that he was the king of the most powerful nation on earth, and knowing how unstable political regimes were (just as they are in our time), King Nebuchadnezzar evidently began to wonder who would succeed him as the world's next great leader. He wondered, in the passion of his megalomania, what would happen to his kingdom when he passed on, and who would succeed his magnificent political reign. So, with these questions on his mind as he retired one evening, King Nebuchadnezzar dreamed a dream of significant import. To the king's amazement and chagrin, he could not remember the dream upon his wakening the next morning. He could only sense that it was an important message that needed to be both remembered, and interpreted.

So King Nebuchadnezzar, upon waking from his sleep, assembled his command of assorted wise men, enchanters, magicians, and astrologers to pool their resources to both recall and interpret his dream. King Nebuchadnezzar told them that he could not remember anything that he had dreamt, and that if they could not help him remember, they would all be put to death. It was Daniel, Shadrach, Meshach, and Abednego who were members of this celebrated and elite coterie. None was able to discern this enormously and spiritually significant dream, save the Prophet Daniel. As providence provided, Daniel was told by God that He would reveal to him the contents of

---

source of knowledge. Christian metaphysics holds that all knowledge emanates from God. Christian metaphysics holds that if we explore for knowledge in a rather speculative manner, we might gain insight, as is the case in this work, into the prescriptive terms of the mystery of God.

the king's dream, and that He would also give him the interpretation thereof. So Daniel went to the king and told him precisely that. He told him that he would pray to God during the night. And he told the king that he would return the next day with the answers he desired. Naturally, having exhausted all other means of gaining the information he desired, King Nebuchadnezzar unwittingly enlisted the divinely inspired interpretative skills of the Prophet Daniel. The next day, then, and in the presence of King Nebuchadnezzar, Daniel spoke thus:

> *No wise men, enchanters, magicians, or astrologers can show to the king the mystery which the king has asked, but there is a God in heaven who reveals mysteries, and he has made known to King Nebuchadnezzar what will be in the latter days* (Daniel 2:27-28, RSV).

Daniel 2:28-45 then records Daniel's recollection and interpretation of King Nebuchadnezzar's dream, quoted in part at the beginning of this chapter. In that dream God revealed to King Nebuchadnezzar who would replace him in the many years after his death. Daniel, having fulfilled the obligation of the king's demand for recalling and interpreting his dream, thereby satisfied a megalomaniac who would have most certainly put to death all of the enchanters, magicians and astrologers had he not done so.

Of particular importance to Christians looking toward the *end times,* is verse forty-four which prophesies the establishment of the final, eternal, and divine kingdom that would last forever, that would eventually replace the last, man-made kingdom (referred to as the ten-nation federacy) mentioned in King Nebuchadnezzar's dream:

> *And in the days of these kings [the ten-nation federacy] shall the God of heaven set up a kingdom, which shall never be destroyed: and the kingdom shall not be left to other people, but it [the eternal kingdom of God] shall break [the other kingdoms] in pieces and consume all these kingdoms [the ten-nation federacy], and it [the eternal kingdom of God] shall stand forever* (KJV).

King Nebuchadnezzar's dream of the final and eternal kingdom that would eventually replace the last, man-made kingdom on earth is the eschatological kingdom of God that is to be established at the end of human history as we shall know it, that is actually and literally to become the governing authority of all that takes place *under the whole heaven* (Daniel 7:27). In chapter one of this book the Manchild was also identified as the eschatological kingdom of God now in the process of being assembled. The Manchild is the eschatological kingdom now in the process of being formed. The kingdom identified as the Manchild is to be established after the end of human history as we know it. The Manchild as the future kingdom of God will actually and literally become the governing authority of all that takes place *under the whole heaven*. King Nebuchadnezzar's dream of the final and eternal kingdom of God is the adumbration of the Manchild found in Revelation 12:5. The dream of King Nebuchadnezzar was a vision given by God of the final, eternal, and everlasting kingdom of God. The Manchild of John the Revelator was also a vision given by God of the final, eternal, and everlasting kingdom of God. This is no mere coincidence. We cannot simply jettison this similarity. Instead we must explore the possibility that God is attempting to tell us something that is so incredible and iconoclastic that it would cause in us the response to sit erect and pay full attention. Indeed, such an exploration reveals that the adumbration in Daniel of the Manchild in the Revelation to Saint John is more than just the foreshadowing of the final and everlasting kingdom of God. It adumbrates what is popularly called *the rapture,* which we shall implicate in various places throughout this work, but will be transfixed in chapters 5-7.[5] It also adumbrates what the New Testament continually calls *the mystery* of God, which we will discuss in the next chapter.

---

5. In addition to chapters 5-7, Appendix I presents a study of what is popularly known as *the Second Coming* of Christ.

3

God's *Mystery of the Ages*

For this reason, I, Paul, a prisoner for Christ Jesus on behalf of you Gentiles—assuming that you have heard of the stewardship of God's grace that was given to me for you, how the mystery was made known to me by revelation, as I have written briefly. When you read this you can perceive my insight into the mystery of Christ, which was not made known to the sons of men in other generations as it has now been revealed to His holy apostles and prophets by the Spirit, that is, how the Gentiles are fellow heirs, members of the same Body, and partakers of the promise in Christ Jesus through the gospel. Of this gospel I was made a minister according to the gift of God's grace which was given me by the working of His power. To me, though I am the very least of all the saints, this grace was given, to preach to the Gentiles the unsearchable riches of Christ, and to make all men see what is the plan of the mystery hidden for ages in God who created all things; that through the Church the manifold wisdom of God might now be made known to the principalities and powers in the heavenly places. This was according to the eternal purpose which He has realized in Christ Jesus our Lord.

—The Apostle Paul (Ephesians 3:1-12, RSV)

In chapter one, the identity of the Manchild was unveiled through the medium of a discourse reflecting a conflation of Scripture and reason. In chapter two, the adumbration of the Manchild was made

---

manifest through the similar agency of conflating Scripture and reason. In chapter four, we want to ponder the significance of the adumbration as it relates to what is popularly called *end times* theology. But in this chapter, we want to contemplate the concept of *the mystery of God* as it relates to what philosophers call *the metaphysical question,* namely, *Why is there the mystery of God in the first place?*

As has already been faintly suggested in the previous chapter, something truly incredible and iconoclastic is taking place even now in the process of the evolution of what the Scriptures refer to as the mystery of God. This mystery, just seen in the previous chapter, is adumbrated by the revelation of the succession of kingdoms in King Nebuchadnezzar's dream. But knowing that the mystery has its adumbration in the Book of Daniel is like telling a young child *I told you so* when he reaches out to the hot stove and burns himself for the first time: We know that it hurts only *because we ourselves have been burned.* From the child's perspective, he has not yet accumulated sufficient experience to learn *a posteriori* that touching a hot stove will inflict pain. To human beings living in the ages of the old testament, the adumbration of the mystery of God found in the Book of Daniel (itself a major piece of the revelation of the apocalyptic puzzle) was *purposefully* not visible. Indeed, according to God's timetable, it was not until the time of the New Testament that sufficiently prodigious pieces of the apocalyptic puzzle were unveiled. Paul stated in the opening Scripture quoted at the beginning of this chapter that the mystery of God is that *which was not made known to the sons of men in other generations as it has now been revealed to His holy apostles and prophets by the Spirit* (Ephesians 3:5, RSV): In this we catch a glimpse of the process of the evolution of the mystery of God; in this Scripture we witness the unfolding of the timetable of God which He deemed necessary to unveil a little further His plan *for the fullness of time* (Ephesians 1:10, RSV). Possessing the newly revealed pieces of the apocalyptic puzzle as the New Testament-bound purveyors of the Holy Scriptures did, the adumbration was more than likely not even visible to *them.* But for us, it is. Again, we hold a distinct advantage, this time over both the Old and New Testament prophets, by now holding in our hands the entire revealed word of God. With this revealed word of God, we are now able to peer through it for the purpose of interpreting all that has transpired before us. We have been able to identify the adumbration in the Book of Daniel because we have been given the necessary clues which come from the writings of the New Testament. We are able to grasp the adumbration only because of the distinct advantage we enjoy of being able to view the Old Testament through the paradigm of New Testament revelation. We are therefore able to identify the faint outline of the Kingdom of God to come in the Old Testament only by reading about its near-thorough disclosure in the New Testament. Nearly two thousand years have elapsed since the time of Christ and the concomitant revelation of the mystery of God to the Apostle Paul. God has not yet finished unveiling the pieces to the apocalyptic puzzle. Indeed, the Holy Scriptures tell us that as *the end* approaches, more and more will be revealed about God's plan for the fullness of time. Read again the words of the New Testament Prophet Luke:

And in the last days it shall be, God declares, that I will pour out my Spirit upon all flesh, and your sons and your daughters shall prophesy, and your young men shall see visions and your old men shall dream dreams (Acts 2:17, RSV).

And in the penult discourse of God's written revelation to man it says:

Blessed is he who reads aloud the words of the prophecy, and blessed are those who hear and who keep what is written therein for the time is near (Revelation 1:3, RSV).

From our perspective, as the end draws nigh (which probably is very soon), more and more pieces of the apocalyptic puzzle will be (and are being) revealed through the simple agency of human understanding ameliorated by the reverent attendance upon both the public and private study of the Holy Scriptures. We do not, of course, refer to that purported body of knowledge claimed to be in existence by the heretical sects known as the Gnostics. We simply refer to an understanding which is available for all who diligently and impassionately apply themselves to disciplined studies of the word of God. Like *His holy apostles and prophets* to whom *it has now been revealed,* we are now able to discover, with such impassioned, repetitious, and diligent biblical discipline, further details about the mystery of God, such as the adumbration of the Manchild in the Book of Daniel, which were not visible even to the Apostle Paul. But more importantly, like *His holy apostles and prophets* to whom *it has now been revealed,* we also are now able to discover, with the same impassioned, repetitious, and diligent biblical discipline of Bible study, answers which heretofore stultify all hypotheses promulgated on the concept of the *end times.*[1]

So what, then, is the mystery of God? In what follows is an attempt to establish perspicuity surrounding the understanding of the concept of the mystery of God.[2] To that, let us now turn our attention.

Defining the Mystery of God

The definition of the mystery of God necessarily contains two integral components, namely, a descriptive element and a prescriptive element. The descriptive element simply expresses the mystery's quality and character, employing that common and conventional

---

1. We should therefore pulsate, however ambivalently, with excitement that we are now living in a period of time when even a further unveiling of the mystery of God than that during the time of the Apostle Paul is now taking place regarding what shall eventually become the apocalyptic realization of the eternal kingdom of God. Our ambivalence, no doubt, should emanate from the fact that this greater and final unveiling of the mystery of God necessarily signals the very closing of human history as we now know it. It should therefore become incumbent upon us to investigate thoroughly the concept of the mystery of God. Indeed, the intrigue surrounding it should serve to encourage us to seek out an understanding of all that we can regarding it.
2. For the more initiated, or for those who may have an interest, Appendix II contains a word study on every occurrence of the word *mystery* as it appears throughout the entire Bible. From a casual reading of that word study alone, anyone with even an inkling of a detective's insight should notice that whatever the mystery is, something amazing is certainly talking place. The word occurs only twenty-seven times in the New Testament, with the preponderance of occurrences referring explicitly to the mystery of God. In the Old Testament, the word *mystery* occurs only eight times, interestingly occurring only in the Book of Daniel, all of them referring explicitly to the mystery of God.

means of communication wherein a thing is simply described, like the reporting of the colors contained in a rainbow after a fallen rain. The descriptive element of definition, however, does not entertain the question of the meaning of the rainbow; neither does it ask why there are any rainbows at all. (This is not to be confused with the question concerning the laws of physics, namely, how do rainbows occur?) The duty of the prescriptive element of definition, however, is to answer the Why? question. The prescriptive element of the definition of the mystery of God answers, Why is there the mystery? or Why did God devise the mystery in the first place? Answering these kinds of questions has typically been delegated to those persons who are associated with that area of the soft sciences known as philosophy, but a specialized field within philosophy known as *metaphysics*. The prescriptive element of the mystery of God therefore necessarily concerns itself with what philosophers call the metaphysics of the mystery; namely, Why did God decide in the first place (the metaphysical question), *before the foundation of the world* (Ephesians 1:4, RSV) to devise *a plan for the fullness of time* (Ephesians 1:10, RSV) which would eventually became known as the mystery of God?

The descriptive element is, by comparison, much easier to recount. The following brief presentation of the descriptive element of the mystery of God is not intended to provide anything new, exciting, or of a particular noteworthiness which has not already been stated by previous scholars. It is simply a brief but necessary summarization of what is already commonly accepted as biblical truth. Next we will turn to the discussion of the prescriptive element of the mystery of God, the real heart of this chapter.

The Descriptive Element of the Mystery of God

As we have alluded to earlier, and that which also is reflected in the Scripture quoted at the beginning of this chapter (Ephesians 3:1-12), the mystery of God is the hidden, eternal plan of God which has been, and now is, being revealed to His people in accordance with His purpose which He set forth in Christ (Ephesians 1:9). The mystery of God is the revelation of His plan of salvation for those who would truly be His people. The gospel of the good news of the possibility of eternal salvation in Christ is itself *a mystery which was kept secret since the world began* (Romans 16:25, RSV). The gospel is *the word of God fully known, the mystery hidden for ages and from Angels and men but now made manifest to His saints* (Colossians 1:25-26, RSV). The mystery of God also refers to a secret that had been hidden until the time of Christ, but which was subsequently and partially revealed by God to His servants through His Spirit. It is not a secret to be withheld, but one to be shared with all who would come to the knowledge and possession of saving faith in Christ (1 Corinthians 4:1). The mystery of God consists in not only a previously hidden truth which has been and now is presently divulged, but it consists in a supernatural element which remains yet unrealized in our time: the realization of the eschatological city of God, the new Jerusalem. The mystery of God is His plan to populate the new Jerusalem with earthly creatures who have been created in His image. It shall come to pass that,

> *in the days of the trumpet call to be sounded by the seventh Angel, the mystery of God, as He announced to His servants the prophets, should be fulfilled* (Revelation 10:7, RSV).

Various scholastic biblical works have summarized the parts of the mystery in the following aggregate fashion:[3]

1. The Mystery of the Kingdom of Heaven (parallel occurrences in Matthew 13:11; Mark 4:11; Luke 8:10).
2. The Mystery of the Resurrection of the Saints at the end of human history as we now know it (1 Corinthians 15:51,52; 1 Thessalonians 4:14,17).
3. The Mystery of the Church as the Body of Christ whose constitution will include Jews and Gentiles (Ephesians 3:1-11; 6:19; Colossians 4:3).

---

3. See, for example, the definitive biblical references such as Unger's Bible Dictionary (Moody Press), Nelson's Illustrated Bible Dictionary (Thomas Nelson Publishers), or The Oxford Dictionary of the Christian Church (Oxford University Press). This information is nothing new. It is commonly accepted as biblical fact. Nevertheless, it would never hurt to examine the primary sources.

4. The Mystery of the Church as the Bride of Christ (Ephesians 5:28-32).

5. The Mystery of Christ in us (Galatians 2:20; Colossians 1:26,27).

6. The Mystery of God as Christ (Colossians 2:2,9; 1 Corinthians 2:7) involving God as Christ as the fullness of God in corporeal.

7. The Mystery of the Lawless One (2 Thessalonians 2:7; Matthew 13:33).

8. The Mystery of Restoration, in which man is restored to godliness (1 Timothy 3:16).

9. The Mystery of Israel's blindness in the Gospel age (Romans 11:25).

10. The Mystery of the Seven Stars (Revelation 1:20).

11. The Mystery of Babylon the Harlot (Revelation 7:5,7).

The above outline of the details of the mystery of God is common knowledge. It is a simple portrayal of biblical texts as they pertain to the quality, character, and meaning of the mystery of God. There is no lack for the understanding of the descriptive element of the definition of the mystery of God. There is, however, sufficient want of understanding for the prescriptive element of the definition of the mystery of God. To that, which the rest of this chapter is now devoted, let us now turn.

The Prescriptive Element of the Mystery of God (Part I)

Why would a plan to populate an eschatological realm called heaven be subsumed and kept secret under the rubric of the mystery? Why would this mystery remain hidden until the first advent of Christ? Why did God devise in the first place the plan contained, hidden, and subsequently revealed in the concept of the mystery?

The answers to these questions will not only be more difficult to ascertain than those within the descriptive element, but they will be more difficult to defend as well. This will be the case for two reasons. One, because it is one thing to merely report the apparent objective facts of the colors emanating from the rainbow after an evening rain, and quite another thing to speculate about the motives of anyone, let alone God, as we will be doing here. Two, the metaphysical aspect of this inquiry is, by definition, an inquiry into the first occurrences of events which occurred many, many, many millennia before the human race even existed. We were not present when it took place. We therefore can but put forward only an educated and informed best guess to explain the events about which we are inquiring. It is, indubitably, a two-edged sword. It is an area of both speculation and metaphysical philosophy, appropriately labeled, *speculative metaphysics*.

This does not mean that the answers to the metaphysical questions queried above are unavailable, or that the answers given below will not be correct. It simply means that their ascertainment and defense will not be so "black and white" as would be the simple reporting of the colors of the rainbow. Indeed, the prescriptive element of the definition of the mystery of God is one which transcends the more black and white orb of factual knowledge: it is speculative. Speculation is nevertheless the necessary *modus operandi* for answering these kinds of questions, the metaphysical questions.

The answers will be, then, by definition, beyond the limits of human experience. The questions cause us to speculate about the interior thought processes of God almighty, when we could not possibly know what He was thinking at the beginning of time. This quest for the answers to the metaphysical questions, then, must remain speculative, which means that conclusions, evolving as they will from the indulgence in conjectural thought, must remain tentative at best. It also means that it is not an argument easily defended by *prooftexting*, or by the quoting of prodigious quantities of Scripture. It is therefore an area which easily lends itself both to greater critical review and to greater apologetic difficulty.

It really doesn't matter that it is an area which easily lends itself to greater critical review and to greater apologetic difficulty, because the minor hypothesis contained in this section is not essential to the overall hypothesis of the Manchild. Rather, this discussion of the prescriptive element of the definition of the mystery of God is provided for those certain curious intellectual types who might be titillated by questions of what is otherwise known as the *first causes,* the genesis of humankind, and God's purpose contained therein. But no matter the extensiveness of critical review this section might receive, and no matter the inherent apologetic difficulty contained therewith, there shall nevertheless remain the empirical fact that there exists the revealed mystery of God. There is no question concerning this. Indeed, whether or not this section hits the mark in correctly evaluating the motives God may have had for the introduction of a plan for the ages of time, we shall still possess what the Scriptures refer to as the mystery of God. The potential lack of veracity in this section, then, in no way denigrates the apocalyptic prediction that Jesus shall one day return (1 Thessalonians 2:7) and thereinafter reign as the head of an eschatological council which shall rule the world. So, having said that, let's forge ahead knowing we are on enchanted, speculative ground!

Ad Rem

Genesis 1:1 begins with the words, *In the beginning* . . . Conventional wisdom dictates that this is the first recorded recognition of time in what would become an immediate succession of sequential events in the history of mankind which descended from Adam and Eve. Archbishop Ussher, a scholar of the early seventeenth century, set himself to calculate the exact number of years from the point of this creation of the race homo sapiens to the time of Christ. His calculation determined that Adam must have been created in 4004 B.C. Hence, adding the years since the time of Christ to the present, there would be approximately six thousand years to the age of mankind as we know it. However credible we desire this piece of factual evidence to be; however prodigious our desire it is for it to fit into the realm of secular scientific authenticity, we are, in essence, akin to the infamous American military figure, General Custer, who nobly defended his ground *till death [him did] part*. Read the rather fundamentalist critique of Archbishop Ussher's findings:[4]

"[T]he compressed chronology of Archbishop Ussher, who assumes unbroken succession of father-son relationship in the genealogical lists of Genesis 5 and 11, and who places the creation of man around 4000 B.C., is untenable in the light of attested archeological facts."

---

4. Unger's Bible Dictionary (Chicago: Moody Press, 1974), p. 202.

While the range of years numbering the longevity of the race *homo sapiens* is 4000 to 10,000 years,[5] we are still left in a quandary of sorts regarding the geological evidence of the earth's existence which dates the creation of the earth back to millions of years ago.

For example, there are many geological formations scattered throughout the world where horizontal layers, upon horizontal layers, upon horizontal layers of sediment can be observed, each layer reflecting a chronological period in itself in the life of the earth. In many, many of these geological formations, one need only estimate the date of the formation by counting the layers present. It is not then difficult to antedate these formations to the creation of Adam and Eve, far exceeding a million years.

Or take fuel oils, like coal and oil, which also are called fossil fuels. Fossil fuels are nothing more than degenerated living creatures whose structures have for so long decomposed that their forms are totally unrecognizable. It takes millions of years for living creatures to lay compressed beneath the earth before they assume the form of fossil fuels, usable to power our machines.

Or take the archeological discoveries of bones of prehistoric men, women, and animals. Although carbon 14 dating is not as exact as some would like it to be (even if it were off by a factor of ten thousand years), we must still reckon with a dating system determined by it which indicates that these bones existed many, many millennia before even the earliest allowable date of the Creation of Adam and Eve.

What then are we to say? Before you drop this book and run for fundamental cover, be advised that the theory of creation shall prevail! We need only look at the first two verses of the Book of Genesis to vindicate the theory of creation, and to adjudicate the peddlers of the subtle and tricky, but beguiling and generally fallacious method of reasoning known as the theory of evolution. Let us give you the findings.

---

5. B. C. Byron Nelson, a conservative scholar, argues for an even greater antiquity of man in *Before Abraham, Prehistoric Man and Bible Life* (Minneapolis, 1948, p. 95). But this still cannot reckon the incontrovertible fact that the earth's fossil records indicate an age in the millions.

The Findings

While the early chapters of the Book of Genesis give us no date for the creation of the world or of man, Genesis 1:1 puts the absolute origin of the universe in the dateless past, which itself allows for all of the ages outlined by the geological sciences. In Genesis 1:1, God created the heavens and the earth. But in Genesis 1:2 we read that the earth which God had created in verse one had become empty and void. Isaiah 45:18 reads:

> For thus says the LORD, Who created the heavens (He is God), Who formed the earth and made it (He established it; He did not create it a chaos, He formed it to be inhabited!): "I am the LORD, and there is no other" (RSV).

Something happened between verse one and verse two. In Genesis 1:1 God created the earth not in chaos, but to be inhabited, yet in the very next verse the earth is chaotic, it is without form, and it is void. The Hebrew word for earth in verse one is *erets*, meaning *dry ground*. So it could read, *In the beginning God created the heavens and the dry ground*. But in verse two the earth is covered with water; it is now a wet land instead of a dry land. Read, then, the words of the Old Testament Prophet Jeremiah, under the influence of the Spirit of God:

> I looked on the earth, and lo, it was waste and void; and to the heavens, and they had no light. I looked on the mountains, and lo, they were quaking, and all the hills moved to and fro. I looked, and lo, the fruitful land was a desert, and all its cities were laid in ruins before the LORD, before His fierce anger (4:23-26, RSV).

Jeremiah was given a vision by God of the total destruction of life on earth, with the *waste and void* chillingly reminiscent of Genesis 1:2's *without form and void*. Jeremiah had been given the vision of the total destruction of the world in order to make a contrast between the entire earth being totally desolate, and the land of Israel being partially desolate. God's purpose in Jeremiah's vision was to let Israel know that God had previously and utterly cursed the entire earth because of its sin. He wanted to convey to the chosen nation of Israel that He would also make the land of Israel desolate because of their sin. God's promise was that he would never totally desolate the earth again like He had allowed in the ageless past:

The whole land [of Israel] shall be a desolation; yet we will not make a full end [of the rest of the earth] (Jeremiah 4:27, RSV).

What is more startling about the account in Jeremiah is that the absolute total earthly desolation must have occurred before the time of Noah:

Then Noah built an altar to the LORD, and took of every clean animal and of every clean bird, and offered burnt offerings on the altar. And when the LORD smelled the pleasing odor, the LORD said in His heart, "I will never again curse the ground because of man, for the imagination of man's heart is evil from his youth; neither will I ever again destroy every living creature as I have done. While the earth remains, seedtime and harvest, cold and heat, summer and winter, day and night, shall not cease" (Genesis 8:20-22, RSV).

From this account in Genesis, we know that the time of Jeremiah's vision of the total destruction of all that lived must have preceded—by necessity—the promise of God to Noah, because God promised that after the Noahic flood He would never repeat the same process. So Jeremiah's vision certainly could not be that of the Noahic flood, because after the flood, according to the Book of Genesis, there was still life remaining over the face of the earth:

He blotted out every living thing that was upon the face of the ground, man and animals and creeping things and birds of the air; they were blotted out from the earth. Only Noah was left [and the animals upon the ark], and those that were with him in the ark (Genesis 7:23, RSV).

But in Jeremiah's vision, there was absolutely no life left. His vision therefore must antedate the Noahic flood. But we also know that there has never been a time since the Creation of Adam and Eve when the earth was desolate and empty, or a waste and ruin, by simply examining the Scriptures. Indeed, such an examination shows that there never has been a time since the Creation of Adam and Eve when the heavens had no lights shining on earth, or when there was no man, no birds, no cities, and no fruitful places. There never has been a time since the Creation of Adam and Even when the whole world was a wilderness and all the cities were broken down. Hence, we are therefore led to the incontrovertible conclusion that the total destruction of all that was living upon the earth in the vision of Jeremiah must have taken place before the Creation of Adam and Eve.[6] Read then, the words of the Apostle Peter:

> *This is now the second letter that I have written to you, beloved, and in both of them I have aroused your sincere mind by way of reminder; that you should remember the predictions of the holy prophets and the commandment of the Lord and Savior through your apostles. First of all you must understand this, that scoffers will come in the last days with scoffing, following their own passions and saying, "Where is the promise of His coming? For ever since the fathers fell asleep, all things have continued as they were from the beginning of creation." They deliberately ignore this fact, that by the word of God heavens existed long ago, and an earth formed out of water and by means of water, through which the world that then existed was deluged with water and perished. But by the same word the heavens and earth that now exist have been stored up for fire, being kept until the day of judgment and destruction of ungodly men* (2 Peter 3:1-7, RSV).

Finis Jennings Dake pontificates on this portion of Scripture:

"Two social systems are mentioned here by Peter: one was *before* the one *which is now,* and the other, *after* the one *that then*

---

6. For those of you who are less erudite than other scholars in the biblical theories of the genesis of the earth and the creation of Adam and Eve, this assertion is commonly known as the *gap theory.* It represents nothing which has not been previously suggested by scholars. While it is not the intent of this work to create an apology for the defense of the gap theory (since it is so widely recognized as theory within the ranks of creation history), the reader is invited to obtain and read another, shorter published article by Willard Thomas entitled, *Creation Versus Evolution.* A copy of this article is available upon request.

was (verses 6-7). The former social system perished by water and the present one will perish by fire (verses 6-7). The former social system was created *in the beginning* and was destroyed by the flood of Genesis 1:1-2. The present social system was created in six days since the flood of Genesis 1:2 (Genesis 1:3-2:25). The flood of Noah did not destroy all the social system on earth between Adam and Noah, for some were preserved in the ark to continue that social system after the flood; but the social system *that then was* before the present one utterly perished. Not one man, bird, or animal was left alive (verse 6; Genesis 1:2; Jeremiah 4:23-26). No reference in Scripture can be found of a change in the heavens and the earth in Noah's day, as in Adam's day (Genesis 1:3-2:25). This proves that the world *that then was* had to be before Adam's day because the heavens and the earth, *which are now* came into existence at that time and not at the time of Noah." [7]

What, then, does this mean? It means that the length of time between Genesis 1:1 and Genesis 1:2 was a prodigious one. Psalm 103:8-9 states that:

The LORD is merciful and gracious, slow to anger and abounding in steadfast love. He will not always chide, nor will He keep His anger for ever (RSV).

God must have been very angry to allow the total destruction of all life upon the earth. But since God is so very, very slow at getting angry; and because God's mercy is so plenteous, we must assume that a very long time elapsed before He could no longer continue pouring out His mercy upon that which was living on the planet earth. Indeed, we must assume that the life upon the earth must have been participating in some very great sins (closely approximate to the sin of the world at the time of the Noahic flood), for God to utterly destroy all that was living.

---

7. The Holy Bible, Dake's Annotated Reference Bible, Rev. Finis Jennings Dake (Dake Bible Sales, Inc.: Lawrenceville, Georgia, 1990), p. 274, his emphases. Because Dake's reference Bible contains an abbreviated note system formatted in parallel columns with respective Scripture passages, some liberty has been taken in the above quotation to change the notation markings to facilitate its arrangement here.

So let us draw some conclusions from these findings. First, the time between Genesis 1:1 and Genesis 1:2 must have been a very, very, long time. Second, at some time after the time when *God created the heavens and the dry land*, but before Genesis 1:2, there must have been a total desolation of the planet earth similar to (if it is not one and the same with) that which Jeremiah envisioned. This then would account for the transformation of a world which was with form and not void in Genesis 1:1, into a world which *was without form and void* in Genesis 1:2. But the third conclusion that we can draw from these findings is that there must have existed before the time of Adam and Eve other generations which populated the cities which *were laid in ruins before the LORD* (Jeremiah 4:26, RSV).

A Summary

The heavens and earth were created by God in the ageless past. This is accounted for in Genesis 1:1. Between Genesis 1:1 and Genesis 1:2 there were many, many, many millennia. We know this because God evidently was *pushed to His limits* with the sin He saw in the heavens and the earth that He had created in Genesis 1:1, and when His mercy ran dry, He was provoked to *fierce anger* which caused the total destruction of all life upon the heavens and earth which He had created in Genesis 1:1. God could not easily be provoked to such *fierce anger* in such a short period of time after He had created the heavens and earth in Genesis 1:1. So civilizations prior to Adam and Eve were created and later destroyed; and generations upon generations must have existed before Genesis 1:2, axiomatically before the creation of Adam and Eve. From Jeremiah we know that the earth had been created and destroyed at least once prior to the creation of Adam. How many times before that, only God himself knows.[8] In order to defend the theory of creation, there need only have been one other civilization. In spite of the fact that we cannot know exactly how many times the destruction-rejuvenation cycle continued before the creation of Adam and Eve, we know that there

---

8. There are some things which God chooses not to reveal and thus kept as His secret. See especially Deuteronomy 29:29.

existed at least one world (cosmos) on earth before Genesis 1:2. This fact alone renders the theory of evolution impotent and foolish: archeological discoveries of bones of prehistoric men, women, and animals dating back millions of years ago in no way diminish the reliability and integrity of what the Bible teaches us. Indeed, secular archeological discoveries, in their bittersweet twist of *fate,* have (again) confirmed the story of creation as it is recorded in the Bible: we would expect to find prehistoric bones of men and women and animals dating back before the creation of Adam and Eve. Logic, then, dictates that, from the theory of creation contained in the Scriptures of the Bible, there would be no limit to how old the earth could be: God could have executed the cycle of desolation-rejuvenation only once, as He apparently has done so at least once. But He could have executed the desolation-rejuvenation cycle *ad infinitum* as well.

The Prescriptive Element of the Mystery of God (Part II)

If you have stayed with us this far, you are to be commended. What follows in the next chapter, however, will be an even greater speculation than in Part I of this chapter. It will therefore also tax your cognitive skill. So once again, no matter the extensiveness with which this minor hypothesis misses the mark in understanding God's motive for devising the plan revealed in the mystery, the concept of the mystery still remains an empirical fact in the lives of God's children. Whether or not we understand the mystery, Jesus is still coming back to claim His own. With this disclaimer having been made, let us now turn to the liberty of the indulgence of a splendid conjecture.

4

Why God Put Men and Women
upon the Earth

So I exhort the elders among you, as a fellow elder and a witness of the
sufferings of Christ as well as a partaker in the glory that is to be revealed.
And when the Chief Shepherd is manifested you will obtain the unfading
crown of glory. Humble yourselves therefore under the mighty hand of God,
that in due time he may exalt you. Cast all your anxieties on him, for he
cares about you. Be sober, be watchful. Your adversary the devil prowls
around like a roaring lion, seeking some one to devour. Resist him, firm in
your faith, knowing that the same experience of suffering is required of
your brotherhood throughout the world. And after you have suffered a little
while, the God of all grace, Who has called you to his eternal glory in
Christ, will himself restore, establish, and strengthen you. To him be the
dominion for ever and ever. Amen.

—A Humble Fisherman (1 Peter 5:1, 4, 6-11, RSV)

The Order of Angels, Authorities, and Powers

Throughout the Bible, though sparsely occurring, we can observe
a heavenly *ranking order*. In 1 Peter 3:22 it says that Jesus *has gone*
into heaven and is at the right hand of God, with angels, authorities, and
powers subject to Him (RSV). Revelation 12:7 refers to the Archangel

Michael *and his angels fighting against the dragon; and the dragon and his angels fought.* Job 38:4-7 testifies that God created the heavenly host of angels, archangels,[1] cherubim and seraphim before He laid the foundations of the world. These messengers of angels answered to other similar beings of a higher chain of command. The angels' top commanders are referred to as archangels. In the Bible, interestingly enough, there are only three angels named:[2] Gabriel, Lucifer,[3] and Michael. Gabriel, Lucifer, and Michael were heavenly archangels. And if the activities of each of these are examined in the context of the Bible passages that duly convey their activities, we will be able to discover some intriguing similarities with the triune Godhead, known otherwise as the Father, Son and Holy Spirit. Let us then turn to a

---

1. The New Testament Greek word for archangel means *chief angel*. In the New Testament, the word occurs only twice, in Jude 9 and 1 Thessalonians 4:16. Jude 9 recounts that Michael is the archangel fighting against Satan. In the Thessalonian text, no name is mentioned with the archangel who will signal the descent of the Lord at the rapture.
2. In consideration for Roman Catholic friends, it must be acknowledge that by *Bible* we mean to refer to the canon accepted by Protestants. Roman Catholics devise a system of *seven* archangels, but their documentation comes from extra-biblical sources that orthodox Protestants do not acknowledge as the Word of God. However, some Protestants nevertheless acknowledge the Archangel Raphael. Raphael makes his debut, however, in the same extra-biblical materials, namely, in the Books of Tobit and Enoch.
3. The King James Version, *et al.,* render the Hebrew word *helel* (which means *brightness*) in Isaiah 14:12 as *Lucifer*. Other versions, namely the Revised Standard Version (but *et al.*), translate the same Hebrew word as *Day Star, son of Dawn*. The word *Lucifer* was a Latin word employed by the prodigious scholar Jerome of the fourth century A.D., as well as by other early Church Fathers. The Latin word *Lucifer,* with the use of the word in classical mythology for the planet Venus, means *light bearer*. As we shall see, the history of Lucifer is duly recorded and contrasted with Christ and His body in passages of Scripture such as Isaiah 14:12f, Ezekiel 28:12f, Luke 10:18, 2 Peter 1:19, Revelation 2:26f; 22:16. While nowhere does the Bible explicitly say that Lucifer is Satan, it can easily be deduced from an examination of these Scriptures.

brief examination of the activities of each of the three named angels in the Bible.[4]

The Archangel Gabriel

Gabriel, whose name means *man of God,* confides to mere mortals information regarding the unfolding of the creative order of God. It is in the rabbinical writings that Gabriel is represented as standing in front of the divine throne of God. As the messenger of divine comfort, Gabriel is accorded in Jewish theology the place of highest rank after the Archangel Michael. In the Old Testament, it is Gabriel who is instructed by God to impart wisdom and understanding to Daniel concerning his vision of the final and eternal kingdom of God (Daniel 8:15f, 9:22f), a vision, as we have seen, that adumbrates the final created social order represented by the concept of *the new Jerusalem* in the Revelation to Saint John. In the New Testament, it is Gabriel who informs Zacharias that he shall become the father of John the

---

4. Theologians who possess a keen theological mind may prematurely surmise that what is being suggested by this venture of inquiry is an attempt to justify an heretical theory cleverly subsumed under the rubric of *the economic trinity of God.* But it is not. While the term *economic trinity* is not an unorthodox appellation in theology, attempts to fashion it as the *cause celebre* are unorthodox. The acceptable economic theory of the trinity of God simply refers to a subsection of theology that considers the apparent threefold activities of God. But there are those who wish to limit the triune Godhead to an entity which merely *acts* in different capacities. Ultimately, it is an attempt to deny the deity of Christ. (The roots of this unorthodox theology are found in *modalism,* promulgated by chief exponents like Praxeas, Noetus, and Sabellius. As a form of *monarchianism,* the early church fathers categorically rejected the tenets of this belief system.) The *unacceptable* economic theory of the trinity of God contends that the Son was merely part of an economic trinity who performed duties for God the Father. It maintains that Jesus is not God. We are not at all suggesting anything even remotely close to this. We believe that the triune God *consists in* an economic trinity, but more importantly we believe in an *ontological* trinity, which simply means that Jesus is God (John 10:30), that Jesus is the Holy Spirit (2 Corinthians 3:17), and that (by the law of association) God is the Holy Spirit.

Baptist, again, an announcement participating in the revelation of the final created order by predicting the one who should pave the way for the announcement of Christ who is to be *the head of the body, the Manchild*. And finally, it is Gabriel who informs the Virgin Mary of the special child within her womb (Luke 1:19, 26), this time divulging a most important piece of information regarding who shall become *the head* of the created final and eternal order of the world. It is with the Father of the triune Godhead that we normally associate the creative order of the earth, the source of all that ever was, is, and shall be.

The Archangel Michael

As Gabriel represents the ministration of the angels in the service of men created in God's image, so Michael represents the type and leader of man's strife. Michael acts in the service of God, in the service of His name, and in the service of His strength against the power of Satan. Michael confides to man strength in time of need. In connection with the scriptural and apocryphal passages, Michael was regarded in the early church as the helper of the Christian armies against the heathen, and as a protector of individual Christians against Satan near their times of death. For example, it is Michael who is sent to give strength to the weary and near dead Daniel after his body collapsed while envisioning the things of God (Daniel 10:13f). And it is Michael who stands up to Satan, and by the power of his spoken word, disperses his very presence (Jude 9). Finally, in Revelation 12:7, as we have already referred to in this work, it is Michael and his company of angels who exercise the power of their might against the dragon (and the dragon's angels) to obliterate their forces acting in service against the heavenly hosts of God. Michael, then, represents the power and strength of God, typically associated with the Holy Spirit of the triune Godhead.

The Archangel Lucifer

It was Lucifer who was sent to the earth at the time of the creation of the Garden of Eden,[5] presumably to eventually become the

---

5. Dake says, "No earthly king of Tyre was ever in Eden, as was this angel (Lucifer), nor does this Eden refer to Adam's Eden, although Lucifer was in it also (Genesis 3; 2 Corinthians 11:3). The Eden here was a garden in

caretaker of the civilizations that would inhabit that idyllic place. It is in the Book of Ezekiel that we learn about the Archangel Lucifer:

> *You were the signet of perfection, full of wisdom and perfect in beauty. You were in Eden, the garden of God; every precious stone was your covering, carnelian, topaz, and jasper, chrysolite, beryl, and onyx, sapphire, carbuncle, and emerald, and wrought in gold were your settings and your engravings. On the day that you were created they were prepared. With an anointed guardian cherub I placed you; you were on the holy mountain of God; in the midst of stones of fire you walked. You were blameless in your ways from the day you were created, till iniquity was found in you* (Ezekiel 28:12-15, RSV).

Before *iniquity was found in* Lucifer, he held a position of regal importance as one of three archangels in charge of carrying out the orders of the triune Godhead. He was the teacher, the instructor, the musician, the most beautiful in the day he was created. But he became self-exalted. He attempted to raise his throne one time, one inch, too high. And because of this, God cast him out of the heavens.

From this account in Ezekiel it is obvious that God's intention for Lucifer was for Lucifer to exist over the face of the earth as a guardian archangel (with subordinates beneath him) to watch over mankind. His role was that attached to exercising dominion over the earth. From the following pericope out of Isaiah, we learn not only of Lucifer's downfall, but of his responsibility as the administrator (before his sin) for the second person of the *acceptable* economic trinity:

> *How you are fallen from heaven, O Day Star, son of Dawn! How you are cut down to the ground, you who laid the nations low! You said in your heart, "I will ascend to heaven; above the stars of God I will set my throne on high; I will sit on the mount of assembly in the far north; I will ascend above the heights of the clouds, I will make myself like the Most High." But you are brought down to Sheol, to the depths of the Pit. Those who see you will stare at you, and ponder*

---

the earth when [Satan] ruled in perfection and sinlessness before he fell (verse 13)"—p. 834, see article entitled, Pre-Adamite Eden (28:13).

over you: "Is this the man who made the earth tremble, who shook kingdoms, who made the world like a desert and overthrew its cities, who did not let his prisoners go home?" All the kings of the nations lie in glory, each in his own tomb, but you are cast out, away from your sepulcher, like a loathed untimely birth, clothed with the slain, those pierced by the sword, who go down to the stones of the Pit, like a dead body trodden under foot. You will not be joined with them in burial, because you have destroyed your land, you have slain your people (Isaiah 14:12-20, RSV).

Two things are noteworthy from the two preceding biblical texts. First, Lucifer's sin did not come until after God had appointed him charge over the earth. Second, Lucifer's (partial) preiniquity *job description* within the economic trinity of the Godhead was to lay *the nations* low (verse 12); to make *the earth tremble* (verse 16); and to make *the world like a desert and over[throw] its cities* (verse 17). No doubt Lucifer, even after his sin, having been equipped by God to carry out his responsibilities for the Godhead, to this day continues participating in activities much like he was intended by God to perform (which may shed some light upon the question of God's "allowing" cataclysmic destruction upon innocent people). The pericope in Isaiah no doubt also refers to Satan's post-sin activities, because verse 17b states that he did *not let his prisoners go home.* That is, all who died before the time of this spoken word (before Isaiah's vision), were being held by Satan in a special place the Scriptures continually refer to as Sheol. Only now, under the orders of no one but himself (at least, so he thinks), he operates in a capacity ultimately limited by God.

So when we read in Jeremiah 4:23-27 about what may have been a perplexing text about the destruction of civilizations before the creation of Adam and Eve (chapter three), we need only now look to the archangel responsible for carrying out the orders of God to desolate the earth: Lucifer. And, since we have been able to identify an archangel with each of the three persons of the trinity, namely, Gabriel with God the Father, Michael with God the Holy Spirit, we need only find a place for the only other angel named in the entire Bible (Lucifer) to see over what area of the heavenly hosts he was originally given power, authority, and dominion. And there remains but one: Lucifer must have been the supreme archangel for the second person of the trinity, namely, God the Son![6] So in Jeremiah's vision, when the earth was inhabited and governed by people who were subsequently destroyed along with the earth when it was made desolate, it was Lucifer carrying out the orders from the heavenlies, working as an archangel under the direction of God the Son, obediently carrying out the orders that came as a result of God's *fierce anger* after His patience and mercy were exhausted. When Jeremiah envisioned the desolation of men and cities here on earth—*fruitful places,* the text calls them—Lucifer was acting as the archangel for God the Son. No wonder, then, that Satan is now so hell-bent on destroying the works of Jesus: he is at enmity with his former, immediate superior whom he betrayed, and whom he tried to become like! So because Lucifer tried, once God put him on the earth in the Garden of Eden, to become like God, he was cast out of the garden of God. And with Lucifer went his entire company of subordinate, subservient angels who were also attempting to elevate their commanding officer, the Archangel Lucifer, above the throne of God. And in his rebellion, Lucifer, now the fallen angel of God, would begin to work his evil ills upon the man whom the triune Godhead would eventually[7] create *in our image, after our likeness* (Genesis 1:26).

---

6. The current year is A.D. 1993. *A.D.* is the Latin abbreviation for *anno Domini,* that is translated, *the year of our Lord.* We who live in the age of A.D. have always referred to the trinity as, Father, Son, and Holy Spirit. But that was not the case B.C. (simply the English abbreviation for *before Christ,* and for obvious reasons, not used by Jews). In the beginning (Genesis 1:1), the three persons of the trinity nevertheless existed, but in the Gospel according John, we see that the *Son* was the *Word* (John 1:1). In this section, it would be more appropriate to employ the phrase Father, *Word* and Holy Spirit, but unnecessary. Hence, the more familiar phrase *Father, Son and Holy Spirit* is used with the understanding that it should more appropriately be *Father, Word and Holy Spirit.*
7. There is no way we can ascertain how long after the fall of Lucifer that the triune Godhead actually created Adam and Eve. All that can be said is that Adam and Eve were created after Lucifer was excommunicated.

Summary

God created the spirit world (Colossians 1:15-18) of archangels, angels, cherubim, seraphim, and other celestial beings to exist within a chain of command. The triune Godhead is the supreme moral governor of the universe (Daniel 4:17, 34, 35). Each person of the trinity participated in an *economic* capacity to rule the universe: God the Father is associated with absolute authority, wisdom and knowledge; God the Son is associated with the creative order of the universe; and God the Holy Spirit is associated with power, might and strength. Each of the persons of the trinity possessed at His side a so-called *supreme commander* to carry out the duties associated with His respective economic capacity. For God the Father, there was the Archangel Gabriel. For God the Son, there was the Archangel Lucifer. And for God the Holy Spirit, there was the Archangel Michael.

Before the fall of Lucifer there was absolute harmony in the universe. When Lucifer began to desire to be elevated above the level of God Almighty, he was cast, along with his cohorts, out of the heavenly realm of God's universal harmony. Lucifer thereby became the father of disharmony. He would become the head of this present world-system. He would become the Satan who would be the captor of mankind. He would become the liar of the universe (John 8:44). He would become the prince of the power of the air (Ephesians 2:2). He would become our adversary the Devil (1 Peter 5:8). And he would become the dragon, that ancient serpent, who is the Devil and Satan (Revelation 20:2).

The Problem and Reason for the Mystery

The primary hypothesis contained in this work surrounds exposing the mystery of the Manchild. At the beginning of chapter one, Revelation 12:1-5 was quoted, that portrays the birth of the Manchild. Here again are verses three and four:

> *And another portent appeared in heaven; behold, a great red dragon [Satan], with seven heads and ten horns, and seven diadems upon his heads. [His] tail swept down a third of the stars of heaven, and cast them to the earth. And [the dragon] stood before the woman who was about to bear [a child], that he might devour her child when she brought it forth (RSV).*

We have seen that the Bible names only three archangels, namely, Gabriel, Lucifer, and Michael. It seems reasonable to assume that each was given the responsibility over a third of all of the angels, cherubim, and seraphim. Indeed, the text just quoted above out of the Revelation to Saint John names exactly that fraction, namely, *a third.*[8]

When Lucifer was expelled from the heavenly realm of God, with him went a third of the angels which would become known now as fallen angels. And when Lucifer was excommunicated, God the Father was left with the Archangel Gabriel, and God the Holy Spirit with the Archangel Michael, but God the Son was left with no one. Lucifer, whose name means *day star*, abandoned God the Son. This imagery is applied to Christ by the New Testament writers through the use of irony to convey this message. But remember, an *irony* is a figure of speech wherein the literal meaning of the term is the opposite of that intended. In the verses below, Christ was not *the bright morning star. Lucifer* was:

I Jesus have sent my angel to you with this testimony for the churches. I am the root and the offspring of David, the bright morning star (Revelation 22:16, RSV).

Read another use of irony identifying and mocking the separation of Lucifer from God the Son:

For when he received honor and glory from God the Father and the voice was borne to him by the Majestic Glory, "This is my beloved Son, with whom I am well pleased," we heard this voice borne from heaven, for we were with him on the holy mountain. And we have the prophetic word made more sure. You will do well to pay attention to this as to a lamp shining in a dark place, until the day dawns and the morning star [Jesus] rises in your hearts (2 Peter 1:19, RSV).

---

8. For the less initiated, this is a common interpretation of the metaphorical representation in Revelation 12:4. Indeed, we need only look, for example, at the impeccable scholarly work of Nelson's Illustrated Bible Dictionary to see that it, too, reads, "In his fall from God's favor, Satan persuaded one third of the angels to join him in his rebellion (Revelation 12:3-4)," (Thomas Nelson Publishers, 1986, on the topic entitled, SATAN).

And then finally, to hermetically seal the postulate that the Archangel Lucifer was created for the service of God the Son, we present one more piece of evidence. God the Son remained alone as the figurative Head with no body of subordinates to rule the earth. So God immediately set into motion a plan for the fullness of time to replace the body of subordinates for the Son. That *body* is to be *the church, the body of the Christ,* the body is made up of believers who endure to the end. Revelation 2:26-28 says:

> *He who conquers and who keeps my works until the end, I will give him power over the nations, and he shall rule them with a rod of iron, as when earthen pots are broken in pieces, even as I myself have received power from my Father; and I will give him the morning star* (RSV).

In the kingdom that is to come, those who have remained faithful to the end shall constitute the position once occupied by Lucifer and his host of angels. But that exclusive membership will not begin until the time when the eternal, ruling, reigning body of God is established after the blowing of the seventh trumpet (Revelation 11:15ff); that is, when the woman has completed giving birth to the Manchild. The mystery of God hidden since the beginning of time is to replace that group of angels which acted in service of God the Son as governors of the earth, but who were subsequently, along with Lucifer, thrown out of the heavenly realm by the triune God because of their sin.

But God, being omniscient, knew before the foundation of the world that Lucifer would one day defect from the band of faithful heavenly hosts. He knew from the beginning of time that He would have to replace that group of fallen angels who once served in their capacity under God the Son. So God devised a plan to replace those fallen angels with *the body of Christ,* to give God the Son once again a population of faithful followers who would serve in the execution of His benevolent dictates. That plan, or secret, or mystery, is contained within the understanding of the concept of the Manchild, pointed to by the adumbration of the kingdom to come in the vision of King Nebuchadnezzar. But it is also adumbrated in a passage out of the Book of Luke:

> *"Lord, even the demons are subject to us in your name!" And [he] said to them, "I saw Satan fall like lightning from heaven. Behold, I*

have given you authority to tread upon serpents and scorpions, and over all the power of the enemy; and nothing shall hurt you. Nevertheless, do not rejoice in this, that the spirits are subject to you; but rejoice that your names are written in heaven" (10:17-19, RSV).

Here Jesus recalls the act in the history in the ageless past wherein His supreme commander Lucifer was cast out of heaven. But what is even more remarkable about this text is that Jesus is already adumbrating the new social order that is to come by informing His faithful, devoted followers (who shall rule with Him in eternity), that they are, and shall be, in service under God the Son over the ranks of those who have defected with the fallen Archangel Lucifer.

There is little doubt that Daniel and King Nebuchadnezzar knew that their vision of the successive earthly kingdoms was adumbrating the final, eternal, kingdom of God. And there is little doubt that Daniel and King Nebuchadnezzar would have believed that that final, eternal kingdom would consist of true believers of Yahweh. However, there is also little doubt that neither Daniel nor King Nebuchadnezzar knew that their vision of the final, eternal, kingdom of God reflected the mystery of God to replenish the fallen angels cast out of heaven along with Lucifer. Even within the ranks of the New Testament writers there is little doubt that *they* possessed no knowledge of the replacement theory of fallen angels. The idea of an eternal kingdom of God was certainly ascertainable from the dream of Nebuchadnezzar (at least to one with a Hebrew or Christian eye). What was not visible, however, was that human beings were created to replace angelic beings who had fallen into disrepute. We, living in the age of biblical revelation as we are, are viewing from a distinct advantage point of being able to see in past biblical texts shadows of what is now being revealed.[9] But as we look back over the chronological

---

9. We are acutely aware of the allegory-allegorizing dichotomy within the ranks of hermeneutics. An allegory is a more extensive form of the literary device called a metaphor. An allegory is a story put together with several points of comparison. (For example, the story of the Good Shepherd is an allegory told for the specific purpose of having the door represent Christ; of having the shepherd represent Christ; and of having the sheep represent those for whom Christ laid down His life.) An allegory is a very

developments in Scripture, we can observe only in hindsight, as in the case of the adumbration of the Manchild in the Book of Daniel, that God has revealed but few, and tiny, selected pieces of the apocalyptic puzzle. There is a reason for this.

God in His infinite wisdom knew that He could not let the mystery be fully revealed from the moment of Lucifer's excommunication from the heavenlies. He knew that He could not even let the *principalities and powers in the heavenly places* know of the mystery, because the risk of the discovery of the plan of the mystery by Satan was too great: Lucifer, already drunk with the insanity of the intoxicants of thoughts of becoming like God, would embark upon a truly frenzied and furious rampage against mankind with a violent excitement of a paroxysm of mania, mental derangement and delirium. God knew that revealing too much to even those remaining faithful heavenly hosts before the ascension of Christ would risk disclosing information that most certainly would have brought the wrath of Satan's mania upon God's holy creation. (Indeed, when God elected to reveal what He did to the Apostle Paul, it was only then revealed by no other than God the Holy Spirit Himself, and not His Archangel Gabriel [Ephesians 3:5]).

So it is no wonder that we are able to look back over Old Testament Scriptures and find in their penumbra sign-posts that can now be clearly interpreted as pointing to the mystery of God as we now know it. With the knowledge of revelation that we who live in the dispensation of the Holy Spirit now possess, we are able to see things that God forbade others to see. Once Christ ascended into heaven, the mystery was no longer hidden, though God is not yet finished removing the veil. The veil has been raised only insignificantly, like the beholding groom with his bride before the altar. But Christ has not yet kissed the bride to consummate the marriage, which means,

---

legitimate way of teaching biblical truth and should not be confused with allegorizing. Allegorizing takes a narrative text that was not intended to teach biblical truth by identifying the parts within its story. Allegorizing forces a point by point comparison upon a narrative, thereby conveying ideas different from those intended by the original author. Allegorizing is an arbitrary way of handling a narrative text. We are not here referring to allegorizing.

however tragical, for those of us who are designated *true believers*, that we are now living in the wake of increased demonic activity emanating from a devil who is now also learning of the deeper meaning of the mystery of God. We who are true believers shall become the recipients of attacks of increasing magnitude, frequency, and severity as Satan learns that we shall constitute the body of Christ. Satan, though thoroughly deluded, is beginning to catch a glimpse of the entire mystery of God. And once he does, his fury shall be unleashed in ways that words cannot make hyperbolic.

James Dobson, upon moving his corporate headquarters from California to Colorado, made a speech to his colleagues. In that introductory speech, Dr. Dobson admonished his staff to be wary of intra-corporate attempts to create strife and dissension. He spoke of the agency of the adversary who was on the prowl to destroy their work through *Focus on the Family*. In order to illustrate his point, he reiterated the story of a missionary from Africa.

The missionary, upon returning to his hut adorned with the best possible accouterments of a native civilization, discovered a python in his domicile. He closed the door, leaving the snake inside, to secure a gun from his truck. The gun was loaded with a single bullet. He had no others. So he returned to the hut to kill the intruder. He shot the python, and though the snake was mortally wounded it did not immediately die. The missionary left until the snake had died.

When the missionary returned, he found his place of residence totally destroyed by the thrashing of the dying python. In the wake of the snake's sustained encounter with dying, it had totally shredded every piece of furniture and belonging inside the hut. There was nothing left intact.

The missionary then concluded that a similar scene is now occurring in the world. Satan has been mortally wounded by the Son of God through His defeat of him through His death, burial and resurrection. Satan is only now thrashing around the world in his death dance, inflicting pain and destruction upon the world.

The predictions of Christ Himself were that in the end times there would be a rise in apostasy and occultism, twin peaks of the head of Satan. In the apocalyptic portions of Scripture we read of the unbelievable tribulation that is to come, such that *if those days had not been shortened, no human being would be saved* (Matthew 24:22, RSV).[10] As the Day of Judgment draws closer, Satan will learn more and more of the details of the mystery of God because as the Day of Judgment draws closer (in *the last days*), God will *pour out [His] Spirit* (Acts 2:17) upon young and old men alike who will be given the concluding pieces of the apocalyptic puzzle of the mystery of God. As the time draws nigh, it will be too late for Satan to offer counter measures. He will be left with but one tactic to employ in the service of his anger at being fooled by the wisdom of Almighty God: wrath.

We had better be ready. We had better be in Christ. We had better not be deceiving ourselves about our modern world or the sin which surrounds us on every hand.

---

10. Chapters eight and nine will consider this incredible period for the future of the human race, but only insofar as it relates to the theory of the mystery of the Manchild as promulgated in this work.

5

The Beginning of the Birth of the Manchild

So when they had come together, they asked him, "Lord, will you at this time restore the kingdom to Israel?" He said to them, "It is not for you to know times or seasons which the Father has fixed by his own authority. But you shall receive power when the Holy Spirit has come upon you; and you shall be my witnesses in Jerusalem and in all Judea and Sama'ria and to the end of the earth." And when he had said this, as they were looking on, he was lifted up, and a cloud took him out of their sight. And while they were gazing into heaven as he went, behold, two men stood by them in white robes, and said, "Men of Galilee, why do you stand looking into heaven? This Jesus, who was taken up from you into heaven, will come in the same way as you saw him go into heaven."

—The Acts of the Apostles 1:6-11 (RSV)

The Manchild has been defined in previous chapters as that company of believers which shall comprise the ruling, reigning body of the eternal kingdom of heaven to be established at the end of time. The Manchild is the *magnum opus* of the mystery of God. At its birth, the Manchild shall represent the climax, culmination, consummation, and conclusion of the mystery of God. The concept of the mystery of God is His plan to create the ruling, reigning body to populate the future kingdom of heaven. The concept of the Manchild is the substance of the mystery. The concept of the adumbration predicts the birth of the Manchild contained within the mystery of God. The birth of the Manchild decrees that the mystery of God has been realized *in toto*. The birth of the Manchild signals the completed work of God, heretofore hidden within the concept of the mystery of God, which is to repopulate that vacancy created in the ageless past when a third of the heavenly host of angels was excommunicated from the heavenly realm with the Archangel Lucifer when he attempted to become like God. The birth of the Manchild adjudicates that the final chapter of earthly human history as we currently understand it will have been written. The birth of the Manchild, therefore, is the denouement of the mystery of God, the final disentangling of the intricacies of the plot contained within the mystery of God.

But—to employ similitude of the metaphor employed by John the Revelator—the Manchild has not yet been given full birth.[1] The body—as distinct from the head of the body which is Christ—is still in the figurative womb of the woman who figuratively represents God's chosen people who were destined by Him in the ageless past to comprise the future citizenry of the kingdom of heaven which is yet to come. The body of the Manchild in the womb of the woman consists of the saints who have died before us, and those of us who are now and shall remain faithful to the end of our lives or until the time of the birth of the Manchild,[2] which ever comes first. The body of the Manchild in the womb of the woman is at this time yearning

---

1. While the terms *full birth* and *the body* may appear as conundrums here, their meanings take on significant dimensions as we move along in this chapter and the chapters that follow. In this chapter we will show that Christ, being the head of the body, has already been born, constituting what we will call the first rapture. The birth of the body proper (which chapters six and seven duly consider but in this chapter are necessarily made a separate entity from Christ Himself solely for the purposes of this polemic) has not yet taken place. Hence, the term *full birth* implicates the distinction between the head having been born but the body having not yet been so.
2. A common misunderstanding in this area of discipline known as eschatology is that THE return of Christ is synonymous with His appearing to rapture the saints. It is not. This issue will be addressed in detail in chapter seven.

for the denouement, the final consummation of the mystery of God which shall be requisitioned by the birth of the Manchild. The birth of the Manchild, then, is the realization that we who have endured to the end shall inherit the kingdom of heaven which is yet to come. The birth of the Manchild authoritatively and emphatically ends the social order of this world as we know it, but concomitantly beckons the beginning of the new eternal social order among those called out ones whom God foreordained from the beginning of time for those who would constitute His faithful followers. And this new social order, as we already have alluded to, shall be represented by the kingdom of heaven under the dual authority of Christ and His body; a body that, as we have also already noted above, consists of those who have endured to the end, remained faithful to the end, and who have done the will of God to the end. The birth of the Manchild is the quintessential event ushering in the dawn of the new age of the kingdom of God. The birth of the Manchild is, then, by the law of association, synonymous with that eschatological event popularly called "the rapture."

The Word Rapture

The word *rapture* occurs nowhere in the Bible, as other key Christian words vital to the vocabulary of the Church also are notably missing, such as *trinity* (referring to God in three persons), *second coming,* or *membership*. This does not, however, in any way denigrate the validity of the truth reflected by their usage.

The word *rapture* comes from the Latin Vulgate Bible word *rapere*, which connotes the *snatching up* or *catching up* found in many English translations. But the meaning of the word *rapture* originally comes from the Greek new testament word *harpazo*, meaning to carry off, to grasp hastily, to snatch up, and to seize and overpower. It is from this word, translated into the Latin Greek New Testament as *rapere*, that we get the English word *rapture*. The word *rapture* connotes an act of transporting resurrected believers and translated believers of the Church into immortal spiritual bodies to be forever with Christ in eternity. While we will deal at a later time with the implications of the rapture, let it here be said that the word itself is a word which has traditionally described the *catching up* of those living saints by Christ to live eternally with God in His presence. In the conventional wisdom and usage of the scholars in the field of apocalyptic eschatology, the rapture therefore refers to that eschatological event wherein living believers will be *snatched up* from the earth into the heavens (translation); and predeceased believers will be resurrected from the dead. While we do not quibble or cavil with what we are calling a parochial usage of this term, we intend to establish in what follows in this chapter and the following chapters, that the rapture, duly subsumed in this work under the rubric, *the birth* is an event which is more than once executed.[3] In this work, the terms *the*

---

3. An oft-repeated aphorism for purveyors of intellectual antiquity is that nothing is new since Plato, so we might as well give credit where credit is due. Oftentimes what appears to be novelty in academic circles is merely an attempt to stem the tide of phenomenological drift called boredom, but it often has a high casualty in the intellectual circles of academia. That is, were an idea induced or deduced (or both) from a rather larger corpus of known intellectual truths, one's novel idea would often become more readily acceptable to that group of human beings which is often labeled "intellectuals." However, should one publish a novel idea which holds little affinity with the acceptable known corpus of intellectual knowledge, a greater amount of skepticism often ensues. *Ad rem*, the idea of multiple raptures is certainly nothing new. While other theologians have postulated various numbers of separate events subsumed under the rubric of the catching up of the saints to be forever in heaven (some as many as eight), we have found a particular intellectual affinity for the great scholarly work of one Professor Dr. Finis Jennings Dake, Sr. His *magnum opus,* Dake's Annotated Reference Bible [Georgia: Dake Bible Sales, Inc., 1990] may be the best-kept secret in all of conservative, evangelical Christianity. Naturally, while Dake's analysis skirts the issues of the concept of the Manchild, he nevertheless posits, as is being done here and *infra,* the occurrence of five separate events known as multiple raptures. Indeed, the paradigm of multiple raptures seems not only to render a great sense of integrity upon what may otherwise be a confusing set of contradictory biblical statements, but duly disentangles the rather complex diversity of Scriptures on the subject otherwise known as the rapture. In the unfolding of the denouement, it may be that the work of such a great scholar as Dake provided the basis upon which future theologians might be able to supply the critical and missing pieces of the mystery of God. For Dake's marginal treatment of the quintet of raptures he decries is demanded by the Holy Scriptures, see in his work page 175.

---

rapture and *the birth* will be used interchangeably to refer to the same, identical event. Christ was raptured as the firstborn of the kingdom of God. And His body shall also in like manner be raptured in the analogy of John the Revelator, in the birth of the Manchild. In this chapter, then, the birth of Christ as the head of the body will be discussed as an alias for the first rapture. In chapter six, the birth of the torso of the body will be discussed as an alias for the Second rapture. And then in chapter seven, the birth of the rest of the body will be presented as occurring through the third, the fourth, and the fifth raptures. In each of these instances, however, the term *the birth* is to be taken as the all-encompassing rubric for the occurrence of multiple raptures to secure by ultimately finalizing the ruling, reigning body of the kingdom of God.

The Rapture Confusion

The concept of the rapture generates so much disputation amongst the learned, as well as nonlearned, that one might be tempted to think that the Holy Scriptures themselves were uncertain about who might be raptured by whom, and when. But the Scriptures inform us that *God is not a God of confusion but of peace* (1 Corinthians 14:33, RSV). This has never been more true than it is now. We believe that neither God nor His Holy Scriptures intend to be confusing. The veritable confusion surrounding the occurrence of the rapture is no doubt due in part to the fact that "the book" has been shut until the latter days (Daniel 12:4). This fact alone exculpates hermeneutical scholars before us. We are not therefore to condemn or criticize too harshly the diligent works of those who have trod before us in this murky water of apocalyptic interpretation. But "the book" of "the time of the end," judging from the large corpus of material now being published surrounding it, appears to have now been opened to allow those of us in the latter days to successfully negotiate what has heretofore been the tide of difficult, puzzling, and perplexing scriptural passages. We believe that God through the Holy Scriptures now desires that His children understand with perspicuity the ordination leading up to those glorious days when the saints who have endured to the end shall be plucked from the earth and placed into the eternal security of perpetual salvation as members in perpetuity of the kingdom of God which is yet to come. Indeed, as has been mentioned already at various points, as the end draws nearer and nearer, more pieces of the apocalyptic puzzle shall be adduced so that he or she who is watching and waiting shall *know that He is near, at the very gates* (Matthew 24:33).[4] We need only employ the simple agency of human understanding to adduce more pieces of the apocalyptic puzzle: an understanding ameliorated by the inspiration of the Holy Spirit, and by the reverent attendance upon both the public and private study of God's Holy Word. Such a repetitious and diligent exercise will yield results which stultify all hypotheses heretofore promulgated on the concept of the future eschatological event known as the rapture.[5]

In this chapter, then, the method of adducing more pieces of the apocalyptic puzzle will be *initially* to augment the information presented in chapter two (the adumbration) by reviewing it through the paradigm of the concept of the Manchild from chapter one. (The final step in adducing more pieces of the apocalyptic puzzle will be discussed in chapter nine.) It was in chapter two that the evidence was presented which established that the adumbration served as a signpost foreshadowing the mystery of God which was subsequently revealed to both the Apostle Paul and John the Revelator. What was not established in chapter two was that the adumbration serves as more than a

---

4. Matthew 24:36 states that *of that day and hour no one knows.* We are not here suggesting anything different. It is worthy to note, however, that when Jesus spoke to His disciples in this text, His disciples had no knowledge of what we know to be the Church. Their questions emanated from a Jewish perspective concerning the nation of Israel, not the Church; when the Bible is examined through the paradigm of the nation of Israel versus the Church, both of these take different paths to a common final fate. See Grant Jeffrey's, *Armageddon* (Ontario: Frontier Research Pub., 1988), especially chapter ten, for further information.

5. Clarity of scriptural understanding shall dramatically increase even more than it already has as we draw even closer to the end. This necessarily means that whatever modicum of clarity of Scripture this work might possess, it very well may be that it will be superseded by an even clearer understanding in the days which follow. Such is the work of God through the inspiration of the Holy Spirit *in the latter days.*

signpost foreshadowing the mystery of God. This chapter will initial-
ize (but conclude in chapter nine) that the adumbration more poignantly serves to clarify what heretofore has been the confusion over
how and when the so-called rapture will take place. In what follows,
then, are the findings of personal, repetitious, and diligent exercises in
both the public and private examinations of God's Holy Word as they
pertain to the rapture of the head of the body of the Manchild, alias
the first rapture, alias, the ascension of Christ.

Another Look at the Prophets Daniel and John the Revelator

We have seen that the visions of the two witnesses and the eating
of the scrolls—inspired by the work of the Holy Spirit, respectively,
in the Prophets Zechariah and Ezekiel—were nothing new in the
vision given to John the Revelator. And we have seen that the interpretation by the Prophet Daniel of King Nebuchadnezzar's dream
adumbrates the birth of the Manchild contained in John the Revelator's vision. So, given that the source of John's vision was the same
Holy Spirit which inspired Zechariah, Ezekiel, and Daniel, it therefore becomes plausible to postulate that these occurrences of similarity naturally suggest to us that God has been, and now is, attempting to provide greater details surrounding the final consummation of
the mystery of God. While this "plausible postulation" may not at this
point appear obvious, it may become so by especially examining the
intriguing relationship between the visions of King Nebuchadnezzar
and John the Revelator. What appears to be more remarkable, then,
than the Zechariah-Ezekiel-John the Revelator similarities, is the relationship between the Prophets Daniel and John the Revelator who
act as the mouthpieces for God; between the visions of the Manchild
in the Book of Revelation, and that of the successive kingdoms in the
Book of Daniel.

It was Daniel who was told to *shut up the words, and seal the book,
until the time of the end* (Daniel 12:4, RSV). But it was John the
Revelator who was given the task of telling what would happen at the
time of the end:

*The revelation of Jesus Christ, which God gave him to show to his
servants what must soon take place; and he made it known by send-
ing his angel to his servant John, who bore witness to the word of*

God and to the testimony of Jesus Christ, even to all that he saw. Blessed is he who reads aloud the words of the prophecy, and blessed are those who hear, and who keep what is written therein; for the time is near (Revelation 1:1-3 RSV).

In the book of Revelation we find the description of Jesus as the great *Alpha and Omega* [6] (1:8; 21:6; 22:13). The use of the phrase *Alpha and Omega* occurs only in conjunction with the idea of the establishment of the final, eschatological kingdom of God. And, as noted earlier in footnote fourteen in the Introduction, apocalyptic literature proper began with the Book of Daniel. Apocalyptic literature proper also ended with the Book of Revelation. The "alpha" of apocalyptic literature is the Book of Daniel. The "omega" of apocalyptic literature is the Book of Revelation: both visions contained within the Books of Daniel and Revelation explicate the future kingdom of God under the authority of the great Alpha and Omega, the Lord Jesus Christ. The Old Testament adumbration of the Manchild revealed that there shall surely be an eternal kingdom of God to come which shall rule the world with absolute authority, to appear after the establishment of the fifth man-made kingdom. This fifth man-made kingdom is represented in the vision of King Nebuchadnezzar by *the feet and toes partly of potter's clay and partly of iron.* We are told in Daniel 2:41 that this kingdom *shall be a divided kingdom,* which many have postulated to be the ten-nation federacy.[7]

---

6. The only other scriptural location where there is even a close approximate to the *Alpha and Omega* paradigm is in Isaiah 44:6, which reads: *Thus says the LORD, the King of Israel and His Redeemer, the LORD of hosts: "I am the first and I am the last; besides me there is no god."* But in this passage, the idea is clearly the rejection of polytheism, and the establishment of monotheism, but not considered to be connected to a future eschatological realization.

7. The concept of the ten-nation federacy is one whose definition is still a subject of great disagreement within the ranks of biblical scholars but, thankfully, insignificant to the scope of the hypothesis contained in this work. (For a rather extensive, timely, and clever hypothesis of this assumed ten-nation federacy, see David Hunt's book, *Global Peace* (Eugene, Oregon: Harvest House, 1990). As mentioned in an earlier footnote in this chapter, it may be that as the time of the close of this age approaches, we may gain greater understanding of even this concept of apocalyptic reality. Time, however, will be the judge of this.

The adumbration in Daniel simply tells us that this so-called ten-nation federacy shall be superseded by the eventual establishment of the eternal city of God, known otherwise as the kingdom of God, which is yet to come.

Like the sports newscaster who is in a constant state of want for appropriate and sufficient adjectives to describe the win-loss records of various teams, it is easy to run shy of sufficient adjectives to describe that final destination for believers who endure to the end—no doubt a casualty of attempting to avoid the bias of phenom-enological drift, known otherwise as boredom. Just to make it clear, however, the following phrases used in this work refer to the same end, namely, the kingdom of God which is to come, which begins with the birth of the Manchild. While some important distinctions will need to be made in the use of certain terms referring to that period of time after the birth of the Manchild, we do not yet infer significant nor pertinent nuances by the employment of such terms as: the kingdom of God, the kingdom of God to come, the kingdom of God which is to come, the eternal, ruling, reigning body of Christ, the New Jerusalem, the city of God, the eschatological kingdom of God, the everlasting kingdom of God, the kingdom of heaven, etcetera.

When the time is appropriate, or the need dictates, we will point out the necessary nuances in these phrases. For now, however, suffice it to say that in the time-line of apocalyptic fulfillment, the birth of the Manchild ordains the advent of eternal life. However, following the birth of the Manchild, there shall be three-and-a-half years of the great tribulation, or what is also known in Scripture as the time of Jacob's Trouble (Jeremiah 30:7). (This may appear as another conundrum here, but it will be explained *in toto* in chapter eight.) After the time of Jacob's Trouble, Satan will then be bound for a millennium. After this millennium, then, the city of God, called the New Jerusalem, shall descend in all of its splendor. So while the phrases *city of God* and *the New Jerusalem* are used in reference to the time after the birth of the Manchild, it must be noted here that these phrases refer to the same specific period in the life of the Manchild. Both of these phrases properly refer to a certain period of time (but not to the immediate period of time) after the birth of the Manchild. They do not specifically refer to the period of time called the great tribulation, nor to the millennium. For now, the above-mentioned phrases shall be employed loosely to simply represent the divine order of God which begins with the birth of the Manchild.

We are at a loss, however, to determine from the text in the Book of Daniel, the actual length of time between the establishment of the last man-made kingdom and the establishment of the eternal kingdom of God. There are no details available in that pericope which might even suggest a specific chronology, though a faint outline of a very crude timetable might be surmised: since there have already been five kingdoms in the last two-and-a-half millennia since King Nebuchadnezzar's dream, it might therefore be assumed that the period of time between the penultimate and ultimate kingdoms will be—or more appropriately, has been—a long time. But then, that pericope out of the Book of Daniel was not intended to divulge a specific timetable. That task was left for another prophet, in another time, through another vision. That subsequent prophet, time, and vision were John the Revelator, in the first century A.D., through the vision of the Manchild. This subsequent and more extensive unveiling of the mystery of God, as found in the Book of Revelation, aggrandizes the sketchy details provided by the adumbration portrayed in the Book of Daniel; it fills in the blanks of the adumbration purposely omitted by God according to the purpose of His plan for the fulless of time.

The vision of the birth of the Manchild in the Book of Revelation is the hermeneutical tool that reveals to purveyors of eschatology some very interesting and intriguing pieces of the apocalyptic puzzle. We perceive from John the Revelator's vision of the birth of the Manchild some rather specific signposts that give testimony of the imminent establishment of the eternal kingdom of God. Compared to that of the adumbration, John's vision encompasses a more specific and truncated period of time. As a matter of fact, John the Revelator's vision is so nearsighted—comparatively speaking—that it represents not two-and-a-half millennia, as has now been the elapsed time of the vision that gave us the adumbration, but just three-and-a-half years. This three-and-a-half-year period immediately precedes that moment of the completed work of selecting the population in the everlasting kingdom of God; it is a period of time which immediately precedes that moment of the closing of the door to eternal life. John's vision of the birth of the Manchild is God's metaphorical vehicle for communicating the consummation of the population of those who will gain entrance into heaven as the ruling, reigning body in eternity!

The visions of King Nebuchadnezzar and John the Revelator, then, if scrutinized and interpreted in light of each other, together become the hermeneutical tool which unlocks more than ever the mystery of the final act of human drama upon the face of the earth. The adumbration-manchild hermeneutical tool will render all previous conundrums involving the rapture divinely perspicacious. While many exegetes have properly understood a good many bits and pieces of the difficult eschatological puzzle, it is the absence of this specific and profound hermeneutical tool that has caused them to miss the bigger picture. The adumbration-manchild hermeneutical tool—which we shall elaborate upon in what follows—presents a thoroughly comprehensive hypothesis that ties together all of the myriad bits and pieces of the apocalyptic puzzle. It has been these bits and pieces in times past that—when taken *in toto*—portrayed contradictory and confusing conclusions. While other scholars have apprehended very specific slivers of the truth of the unfolding events of the end of time, the conclusions emanating from their overall picture have reflected a less than acceptable degree of hermeneutical integrity. In what follows is our attempt to portray an acceptable degree of hermeneutical integrity. We begin by examining the metaphor of John the Revelator.

The Birthing Process

John the Revelator, under the inspiration of the Holy Spirit, extends the metaphorical representation of that eternal, everlasting kingdom of God adumbrated by King Nebuchadnezzar's vision, by equating its advent, epiphany, and establishment with the birthing process. Indeed, while not an unfamiliar concept to readers of the New Testament, John the Revelator equates the ruling, reigning body of the eternal kingdom of God with the concept of a human body. Notice, then, the fleshly metaphorical image of the everlasting kingdom of God in King Nebuchadnezzar's dream:

You saw, O king, and behold, a great image. This image, mighty and of exceeding brightness, stood before you, and its appearance was frightening. The head of this image was of fine gold, its breast and arms of silver, its belly and thighs of bronze, its legs of iron, its feet partly of iron and partly of clay (Daniel 2:31-33, RSV).

The image in King Nebuchadnezzar's dream is also that of a body. That image is being used as a literary device to predict the eternal kingdom of God! Daniel revealed to King Nebuchadnezzar that Nebuchadnezzar represented the head of gold of the image in his dream. He also revealed to the King that the King's dominion stood for the kingdom which was already at hand. But Daniel also spoke of the future kingdoms which would succeed King Nebuchadnezzar. And in Daniel 2:44, Daniel prophesied that during the reign of the fifth kingdom, the everlasting kingdom of God would be established:

And in the days of these kings [the ten nation federacy] shall the God of heaven set up a kingdom which shall never be destroyed: and the kingdom shall not be left to other people, but it shall break in pieces and consume all these kingdoms [the ten nation federacy], and it shall stand for ever (Daniel 2:44, KJV).

But that which breaks the man-made kingdoms of earth which gives way to the establishment of the everlasting kingdom of God is the stone:

As you looked, a stone was cut out by no human hand, and it smote the image on its feet of iron and clay, and broke them in pieces; then the iron, the clay, the bronze, the silver, and the gold, all together were broken in pieces, and became like the chaff of the summer threshing floors; and the wind carried them away, so that not a trace of them could be found. But the stone that struck the image became a great mountain and filled the whole earth. Just as you saw that a stone was cut from a mountain by no human hand, and that it broke in pieces the iron, the bronze, the clay, the silver, and the gold (Daniel 2:34,35,45, RSV).

This stone is the Lord Jesus Christ. In the first letter of the Apostle Peter, Peter says,

Come to him, to that living stone, rejected by men but in God's sight chosen and precious; and like living stones be yourselves built

into a spiritual house, to be a holy priesthood (1 Peter 2:4,5, RSV).

Here we see that not only is Christ the stone, but that the members of His body are also called to be joint heirs with the stone which will *smite the image on its feet of iron and clay, and (break the manmade kingdoms) in pieces,* and set up a kingdom that will become the everlasting kingdom of God. Christ the stone is to be the head of those living stones which are to be built into a spiritual house of holy priests, the body of Christ. So John the Revelator, in the vision given him through the Spirit of God, speaks of the head of the body and the establishment of the everlasting kingdom of living stones:

> *And when He had taken the scroll, the four living creatures and the twenty-four elders fell down before the Lamb, each holding a harp, and with golden bowls full of incense, which are the prayers of the saints; and they sang a new song, saying, "Worthy art thou to take the scroll and to open its seals, for Thou wast slain and by Thy blood didst ransom men for God from every tribe and tongue and people and nation, and has made them a kingdom and priests to our God, and they shall reign on earth"* (Revelation 5.8-10, RSV).

The theme of Christ as the head of the body, the Church, is so common place in the New Testament that it is part and parcel of the Good News of God. The New Testament is prodigiously replete with the recollections on the life of Christ who spent so much of His ministry describing His kingdom and its establishment. Indeed, the New Testament repeatedly identifies Christ as the King of heaven and the head of the body:

> *I do not cease to give thanks for you, remembering you in my prayers, that the God of our Lord Jesus Christ, the Father of glory, may give you a spirit of wisdom and of revelation in the knowledge of him, having the eyes of your hearts enlightened, that you may know what is the hope to which he has called you, what are the riches of his glorious inheritance in the saints, and what is the immeasurable greatness of his power in us who believe, according to the working of his great might which he accomplished in Christ when he raised him from the dead and made him sit at his right hand in the heavenly places, far above all rule and authority and power and dominion, and above every name that is named, not only in this age but also in*

that which is to come; and He has put all things under his feet and has made him the head over all things for the Church, which is his body, the fullness of him who fills all in all (Ephesians 1:16-23, RSV).

And:

Christ is the head of the Church, His body. Christ nourishes and cherishes the Church because we are members of His body. This is the great mystery, and I take it to mean Christ and the Church (Ephesians 5:23,29,30,32, RSV).

And also:

He [Christ] is the head of the body, the Church; he is the beginning, the first-born from the dead, that in everything he might be preeminent (Colassions 1:18, RSV).

Here we not only have the identification of Christ as the head of the body, the Church, but a reference to His preeminence. This theme of the preeminence of Christ and His being the firstborn is developed in other Scriptures as well:

Grace to you and peace from him who is and who was and who is to come, and from the seven spirits who are before his throne, and from Jesus Christ the faithful witness, the firstborn of the dead, and the ruler of kings on earth (Revelation 1:4,5, RSV).

And again:

I will make him the first-born, the highest of the kings of earth (Psalm 89:27, RSV).

Notice then the poignant reference in the Book of Revelation to the head which must first pierce the womb of the woman in the birth of the Manchild:

And to the Angel of the Church in Laodicea write: "The words of the Amen, the faithful and true witness [Jesus], the beginning of God's creation" (Revelation 3:14, RSV).

The Manchild is the *magnum opus* of the mystery of God; it is God's creation *par excellence* to replace the fallen Archangel Lucifer and his unfaithful assistants. The head of the body, as in natural childbirth, appears first. The head which is Christ is therefore the beginning of God's *magnum opus* of the new creature, the Manchild.

Notice, then, the importance of the male who breaks the womb of the woman. Christ, the head of the male Manchild, must be the first-born male of the figurative woman who represents the chosen people of God:

As it is written in the law of the Lord, Every male that openeth the womb shall be called holy to the Lord (Luke 2:23, KJV).

Since John the Revelator was given the vision of the birth of the Manchild as the metaphorical representation of the establishment of the kingdom of God, the birth of the Manchild must necessarily particularize the head being given birth before the body. Not only are normal reproductive births associated with head-first deliveries, but scriptural requirements demand that Christ be the first to enter the eschatological domain we have been calling the everlasting and eternal kingdom of God.

So, as Daniel revealed to King Nebuchadnezzar that Nebuchadnezzar represented the head of the image in his vision, it was apparent that the kingdom representing the head of gold had already been established by King Nebuchadnezzar. This meant that a portion of the vision of King Nebuchadnezzar had already transpired: one of the earthly, man-made kingdoms in Nebuchadnezzar's vision was the kingdom of Babylon, his own kingdom. Similarly, in the case of the vision of John the Revelator, the head which is Christ; which is part of the constitution of the kingdom of God; it, too, has already been born. It, too, in the analogous adumbration of the vision of King Nebuchadnezzar, has already been established. Christ, then, as the head of the body of the Manchild which shall constitute the everlasting kingdom of God has already passed through the birth canal. Christ therefore has already been raptured as a result of the beginning of the birthing process which we said is the quintessential event ushering in the dawn of the new age of the kingdom of God. The birth of the head of the Manchild as Jesus Christ, therefore, represents the first rapture:

> As they [the disciples] were looking on, he [Jesus] was lifted up, and a cloud took him out of their sight. And while they were gazing into heaven as he went, behold, two men stood by them [the disciples], in white robes and said, "Men of Galilee, why do you stand looking into heaven? This Jesus, who was taken up from you into heaven, will come in the same way as you saw him go into heaven" (Acts 1:9-11, RSV).

Christ has already been caught up into the heavens to live eternally in the everlasting kingdom of God for which all of creation is now longing. Christ the stone of King Nebuchadnezzar's dream, in the metaphorical representation of John the Revelator's vision, has already been given birth. The head of the body of the Manchild has pierced the womb of the woman. In the metaphorical medical terminology, the birth is in the stage of delivery known as crowning. The birth of a child is crowning when the head has appeared through the birth canal.

But the body has not yet been delivered. It remains in the womb of the gravid woman who is rapidly approaching parturition. *The body has not yet been raptured, but it is therefore now almost in the very process of being born.* It has been nearly two thousand years since the head has exited the womb. From the time of Nebuchadnezzar's dream we have possessed the vision of the everlasting kingdom of God; a vision subsequently expounded and magnified by the Holy Spirit through His prophet John the Revelator. All of creation history and apocalyptic eschatology points to the realization of this everlasting kingdom. *The number of its inhabitants are being increased daily.* Those who shall become the inhabitants of the eternal kingdom of God are now in the process of being molded, shaped, and refined through fire. They are, to extend John the Revelator's metaphor, now in the process of embryonic maturation in the womb of the parturient woman who is soon to give birth to the new kingdom of God. John the Revelator expounds the climax of the mystery of God as it will be consummated in the birth of the Manchild with the blowing of the last and final seventh trumpet. In Revelation 12:5 the epiphany of the kingdom of God begins; the body of Christ in its entirety is born, and it consists of those who have remained faithful to the end, who endured to the end of their lives, who had been predestined since the beginning of time, and who had therefore remained *in utero* by virtue of their remaining faithful until this moment of the completed birthing process of the Manchild.

It is those who are faithfully fulfilling the will of God who are at this time in the process of being born as part of the body of the Manchild. *The head who is Jesus Christ has already been born. Christ has been raptured.* Our birth, our rapture, is now—through the sequence of unfolding apocalyptic events—waiting in the wings to occur. And when the body in its entirety has been given birth; that is, when the body has been wholly raptured; those who have been faithful shall rule with Christ over the kingdom of God. Read once again the words of Revelation concerning the constitution of the ruling, reigning body of Christ:

> *To him that overcometh will I grant to sit with me in my throne even as I also overcame and am set down with my father in his throne* (Revelation 3:21, KJV).

This ruling, reigning body shall have as its head the Lord Jesus who will govern with absolute authority (Revelation 2:26-27). But—and here's the good news of the Gospel— the eschatological ruling, reigning body shall also be comprised of saints who will jointly govern with this same absolute authority but in subjection to Jesus. After the birth of the Manchild no one will be added to His body. It is the time when the door is shut to eternal life. After the birth of the Manchild no more may enter the kingdom of God.

At the birth of the Manchild the birthing process is completed. The natural birth of a child is also completed only when its feet pass through the birth canal into the world which has already been pierced by its head. In the metaphorical representation of the concept of the Manchild, the head has already been birthed (raptured). The body is now yet in the throes of delivery. We therefore need only examine the scriptural justifications for the various raptures which represent the birthing of the remaining parts of the body, namely, the second rapture in chapter six (the *breast and arms* of silver), and then in chapter seven the third rapture (the *belly and thighs* of bronze), the fourth rapture (the *legs* of iron), and the fifth rapture (the *feet* made partly of iron and partly of clay).

6

What About *After* the Rapture of the Church?

But we would not have you ignorant, brethren, concerning those who are asleep, that you may not grieve as others do who have no hope. For since we believe that Jesus died and rose again, even so, through Jesus, God will bring with him those who have fallen asleep. For this we declare to you by the word of the Lord, that we who are alive, who are left until the coming of the Lord, shall not precede those who have fallen asleep. For the Lord himself will descend from heaven with a cry of command, with the Archangel's call, and with the sound of the trumpet of God. And the dead in Christ will rise first; then we who are alive, who are left, shall be caught up together with them in the clouds to meet the Lord in the air; and so we shall always be with the Lord. Therefore comfort one another with these words.

—The Apostle Paul (1 Thessalonians 4:13-18, RSV)

Early in the previous chapter it was mentioned that the intent of this work was to establish that the rapture is an event which is and will be more than once executed. As we have just seen, the first rapture was determined to be taken as a synonym for the ascension of Christ. We will now turn to what we will be referring to in this chapter as the second rapture, the beginning of the birth of the upper torso of the body, the breast and arms of silver. The second rapture, then, is adumbrated in the Apostle Paul's second epistle to the Christians at Thessalonica:

Now concerning the coming of our Lord Jesus Christ and our assembling to meet him: Let no one deceive you in any way; for that day will not come, unless the rebellion comes first, and the man of lawlessness is revealed, the son of perdition, who opposes and exalts himself against every so-called god or object of worship, so that he takes his seat in the temple of God, proclaiming himself to be God. And you know what is restraining him now so that he may be revealed in his time. For the mystery of lawlessness is already at work; only he who now restrains it [the antichrist] will do so until he [who now restrains the antichrist] is out of the way. And then the lawless one will be revealed (2 Thessalonians 2:1,3-4,6-8, RSV).

While the second rapture must in reality occur during the lifetime of some saints, there is a host of saints which has already died, and will join the living saints at their appointed time with destiny,

The Lord Himself will descend from heaven with a cry of command, with the archangel's call, and with the sound of the trumpet of God. And the dead in Christ will rise first; then we who are alive, who are left, shall be caught up together with them in the clouds to meet the Lord in the air; and so we shall always be with the Lord (First Thessalonians 4:16-17, RSV).

These verses, quoted as the opening Scripture for this chapter, inform us that what is to be called the second rapture, will not only include those saints who are yet living at the time of this supernatural event, but also those saints who have in ages past expired.[1]

---

1. A most interesting and titillating passage occurs in the Gospel according to Saint Matthew. It reads, *And behold, the curtain of the temple was torn in two, from top to bottom; and the earth shook, and the rocks were split; the tombs also were opened, and many bodies of the saints who had fallen asleep were raised, and coming out of the tombs after His resurrection they went into the holy city and appeared to many. When the centurion and those who were with him, keeping watch over Jesus, saw the earthquake and what took place they were filled with awe, and said, "Truly this was the Son of God!"* (Matthew 27:51-55, RSV). It is obvious that this is a perplexing Scripture, compounded by the fact that it is Matthew alone who records it. The

These verses also prescribe a pretribulation[2] rapture for the Church. The beauty and richness of Scripture is that it was written under the inspiration of the Holy Spirit for those who have ears to hear (Matthew 13:9). In this instance, a mild application of noetic rationality upon the inspired word of God establishes the fact of a pretribulation rapture by encouraging us to entertain the following question: Who is now restraining the Antichrist?[3] Three front-runners have been bantered about as likely candidates for this restraining force: the Church, the Holy Spirit, or some form of government. Although some might suggest that "he who now restrains" the son of perdition could very well be governmental agencies or civic structures, let us quickly dismiss this possibility.

The text just quoted out of Second Thessalonians states that the removal of "he who now restrains" will allow the Antichrist to pursue with abandonment his hideous evil. But governmental and social conventions which now sustain the world's political order are not physical entities which can be so easily removed. Therefore, there is nothing to such conventions insofar as they are only human beings which represent and enforce them. Even if it were the conventions *per se* which are now restraining the Antichrist, it would tax the faculties of divergent thinking to imagine such a governmental agency that could wield such moral capacity to stem the tide of evil. (Indeed, it is hard to imagine religious conventions which today yield such sufficient moral restraint to check the growth of demonic acceleration. The anemic success of the Christian pro-life movement is a case in

---

question then becomes, Did these saints then live the rest of their lives until another death? Or, Did these saints also ascend with Jesus at His ascension?

2. Although chapters seven and eight will consider the incredible period in the history of the human race known as the great tribulation, it is nevertheless necessary to refer to this time period until it is more adequately managed in those chapters.

3. The Greek word which is translated "Antichrist" in the English is *antichristos* (an-tee-khris-tos), which simply means "an opponent of the Messiah." *Antichristos* is used only four times throughout the entire Bible, each occurrence contained solely within the two short epistles of the Apostle John (1 John 2:18, 22; 4:3; 2 John 1:7).

point.) So most certainly we must assume that governmental structures will be left intact after the removal of whomever it is which is now restraining the lawless one. In point of fact, so long as there are human beings on this earth, there will always be political conventions employed in an attempt to produce peace, harmony, and stability for commerce, trade, and political intercourse. The Antichrist himself will no doubt use the established social, political and, tragically, the religious systems of the world which will remain after "he who now restrains" him is taken out of the way: the Antichrist will do so in order to catapult his expedient rise to global power. Furthermore, the changes caused by the removal of "he who now restrains," which concomitantly will induce the crisis precipitating the Antichrist's epiphany, will stimulate in those left populating the earth an ever increasing desire for an authoritarian government, if not for what may at first appear to be a very benevolent but totalitarian dictator. Hence, it cannot be social, political, or governmental restraints which are now preventing the "son of perdition," because these conventions will only become exacerbated in the face of a staggering diffidence of a populace which has been left behind in the wake of what is now being postulated to be the second rapture of the saints of God identified as the *upper torso* of the Church.[4]

So there are really only two viable candidates remaining for that position of power which now restrains the Antichrist: either the upper torso of the Church or the Holy Spirit. Here we are needlessly

---

4. We have introduced here a new, more accurate term, *upper torso*. Nebuchadnezzar's dream of the image has five body parts. The head of gold represented his kingdom. The torso of the image consists of an upper torso (the breast and arms of silver) and a lower torso (the belly of bronze). The upper torso represents one kingdom in the succession of kingdoms leading up to the advent of the everlasting kingdom of God. The lower torso represents yet another kingdom in the same succession leading up to the establishment of the everlasting kingdom of God. In the nomenclature of the concept of the Manchild, each of these two body parts represents separate rapture events. As we shall see, the next rapture will be the rapture of the upper torso Church. It will be the lower torso Church that will become the martyred saints of Revelation 6:9-11 during the period of time commonly called the tribulation.

fiddling with an unnecessary semantic because the upper torso of the Church consists of saints who are filled and empowered with the Holy Spirit, and have duly surrendered themselves to the Lordship of Christ. Indeed, the Holy Spirit works through willing human vessels of clay who have emptied themselves of all selfish desires; through those who have indicated a willingness to be filled with the presence of the Most High God for supernatural and miraculous wonders. The upper torso of the Church comprises that select group of people which is *now, at this time* enduring to the end of the age.[5] It is those who are now fulfilling the will of God in their lives. This upper torso Church is, in its constitution, nothing like that spiritual aberration which is well known amongst secular men as a mere physical structure bearing the earthly nomenclature "church," filled in reality with many more nonbelievers than believers (cf. the parable of the wheat and the tares, Matthew 13:24f).

So, to talk about the upper torso Church is to talk about fully devoted followers *ipso facto* they are filled with the Holy Spirit. Indeed, this upper torso Church has always been defined in the words of the following historical apostolic aphorism: "Where the Spirit of the Lord is, there is the One True Church, Apostolic and Universal." To argue that the Holy Spirit could be removed from the Church, thereby leaving behind the faithful followers of Christ who have housed in their earthly bodies the very Person of the Holy Spirit, is not only fallacious, specious, and ludicrous, but it is to break the rules of all rationality and common sense: the Holy Spirit and the Church are like a man and his shadow: where one moves, so does the other. The Church can be taken out of the world such that the Holy Spirit may yet remain in the world, but the Holy Spirit cannot be taken out of the world and yet leave the Church in the world. In the Gospel according to John, Jesus tells His followers that, *I will pray the Father and He will give you another Counselor to be with you for ever, even the Spirit of truth* (14:16,17).

If it is conceded that it is the Holy Spirit who now restrains the lawless one, then it must also be conceded that it is the agency and

---

5. But it is also those who have already died and endured to the end of their lives.

vehicle of the Church through which He now operates. Since the Holy Spirit will never leave the Church, then, if the Holy Spirit is withdrawn to allow the full revelation of the son of perdition, then *ipso facto* the Church must also go with Him. Therfore, "he who now restrains the man of lawlessness" is none other than the Church. The two candidates for the position of the restrainer of the son of perdition are reduced to only one, the Church.

It may be worthy at this point to set the limits of the definitions of certain words which linger in the public mind in a manner virtually meaningless as a result of certain users, and who, in the honesty of the depths of their souls, know that they are not truly representative of the words they employ, but, nevertheless, by reason of arrogance and false hope, seek to gain some semblance of existential peace through the false sense of security generated by hiding behind an appellation which is really inappropriate to their nature, character and integrity. This reference is to the words "Christian" and "believer." This clarification becomes so vital that it truly represents life and death, eternal life and eternal destruction. Matthew 7:13-14 says:

> *Enter by the narrow gate; for the gate is wide and the way is easy, that leads to destruction, and those who enter by it are many. For the gate is narrow and the way is hard, that leads to life, and those who find it are few* (RSV).

Is this simply a literary device of antiquity known as hyperbole? Perhaps. But perhaps not. Read further the words of our Lord:

> *Not every one who says to me, "Lord, Lord," shall enter the kingdom of heaven, but he who does the will of my Father who is in heaven. On that day many will say to me, "Lord, Lord," did we not prophesy in your name, and cast out demons in your name, and do many mighty works in your name? And then will I declare to them, "I never knew you; depart from Me, you evildoers",* (Matthew 7:21-23, RSV).

The amazing thing in this text is that these so called Christians were casting out demons in Jesus' name, and yet they will not get into heaven! The act of spiritual deliverance (exorcism) is the act most associated with pomp and circumstance. But how many thousands upon thousands of people who populate this earth believe that they are going to heaven because they are doing good deeds or good works? *And then will I declare to them, "I never knew you; depart from Me, you evildoers."* In the verses which follow this text, Jesus says,

> *Every one then who hears these words of mine and does them will be like a wise man who built his house upon the rock. And every one who hears these words of mine and does not do them will be like a foolish man who built his house upon the sand* (Matthew 7:24, 26, RSV).

We do not believe that the perfunction of works will get us into heaven; rather, he who obeys the voice of God as it speaks to him through the Holy Scriptures and through his personal daily prayers and devotions will see eternal life. Paul, writing to those who called themselves Christians at Thessalonica, said that two types of people will not make it into heaven. He said that:

> *When the Lord Jesus is revealed from heaven with his mighty angels in flaming fire, [He will] inflict vengeance upon [1.] those who do not know God and [2.] upon those who do not obey the gospel of our Lord Jesus. They shall suffer the punishment of eternal destruction and exclusion from the presence of the Lord and from the glory of his might when he comes on that day to be glorified in his saints* (2 Thessalonians 1:7-10, RSV).

In the Introduction of this work, some rather deleterious characteristics of the body of Christ were cited. The only way to account for the fact that the average, born again, evangelical Christian is spending only an hour a week in the Bible, subscribing to X-rated channels, watching more afternoon soap operas than their non-Christian counterparts, manifesting such a great love for material things that it consumes most of their energy in the pursuit of it, being so prone to a hedonistic lifestyle, and participating in premarital sex is to say that just getting converted is not what Christianity is all about.

It is about attempting to repay God—though it could never be done—for His bountiful mercy in forgiving us for even one of our sins; a single trespass that, without Christ, becomes the sufficient *cause celebre* to send us immediately to hell. It is about attempting to love God for forgiving us on account of His perfect, blemish-free Son. It is about attempting to show God just how much we appreciate His allowing the murder of His only Son as the only perfect sacrifice for our sins. It is about showing our appreciation for that sacrifice by obeying what He commands of us, like a child before his daddy. It is about attempting to hear the voice of God above the world's clamoring which is antithetical to true Christian living. It is about putting aside our own vain attempts at living life and begin living the life that He is asking us to live.

This is the type of devoted follower that God is seeking to populate that eschatological realm in eternity known as the ruling, reigning, body of Christ. Indeed, nothing less than a fully devoted follower deserves to serve in such a regal capacity in tandem with the Lord Jesus as the ruling, reigning, body of the New World Order prophesied by the prophets of old. It is not those who are half converted, still tempted by the foolish and degenerative pursuits of self whom God is seeking for the purpose of populating what will be the New Jerusalem. It is those men and women who are sincerely attempting to *work out their salvation with fear and trembling* (Philippians 2:11-12, RSV). And only you know, my dear friend, in the depth of the honesty of your soul if you are trying to live in two worlds—the world to come and the world which is. We cannot serve two masters. You therefore know whether or not your inmost heart desires with greatest intensity to be pure and holy and sanctified. This book is not about attempting to judge from external compliances of actions normally associated with Christian living whether or not so-and-so is living the deeper life. We are not talking about mimicking an external compliance to the rules, regulations, and laws which have normally been associated with successful Christian living. We are talking about the inner thought life of which no one but you can participate. We are talking about that internal realm of man which only each man and God Himself is cognizant. We are talking about desire, the desire of men and women to love God above any other thing.

Plato discussed what has been called by those who followed him, the Platonic Triangle. Plato asked that if we could place all of the things in life which we desire on the base of the triangle, and begin to stack those things to form a triangle, placing the less important things at the base, and placing the increasingly more important items at the top, what single thing would we place at the top of the triangle? What single thing which we cherish most would we place at the very top of the triangle? For the Christian, it ought to be God, and His righteousness, but it cannot simply be an intellectual ascent. It must be fleshed out in the living of our everyday lives, demonstrated through the works that we do, and that is the works which God Himself is asking us to perform. Sure, casting out demons is a great miraculous work of the Holy Spirit, but has God asked us to do so in such-and-such a person? Sure, devoting our lives to feeding the poor is a great and noble thing, but has God specifically asked us to devote any part of our careers to it? All of us desire at some level to be pure and holy and good, but how much do we desire it? How much we desire the things of God is entirely a function of the human will. Through an act of our wills, through an exercise of our choice, we can choose the things of God no matter how much our flesh desires the things that are not of God. If man were not able to choose and, with the power of the Holy Spirit, overcome "he who is in the world," then Christianity is a great cosmic joke upon a prodigiously deceived human race. God will not coerce us to obey Him. He will not bend our desires against our will. He will not manipulate us into a citizenship in His kingdom. We must first express that depth of desire to be there by obeying His plan for our lives. And when we express this sincere willingness, He then fills us with His Holy Spirit for power and victory. This is the kind of man or woman we would call a Christian. For a Christian is someone who follows Christ. Not someone who follows Christ in most of what He dictates. Not someone who follows Christ most of the time. Not someone who follows Christ when it is convenient, expedient, or safe. But someone who follows Him no matter what the cost. No matter where the path. No matter when the time.

So we come up with terms like "true Christian" and "true believer" to describe the fully devoted follower of Christ. (The latter is a necessary concession anyway because it says in James 2.19 that *even the demons believe, and shudder*. This no doubt puts the atheist in a rather peculiar camp.) A true believer or true Christian is one who is sold out to Christ; one who walks where Jesus tells him; one who goes when Jesus tells him to go; one who does what Jesus tells him, in the small and little things, before the big and great things.

So when the terms "Christian" and "true believer" are used, it should be in reference to that select subgroup of people who have had a conversion experience to the lordship of Christ. Many who call themselves Christian, so the Scriptures poignantly portray, will be precluded from participating in what is here being called the second rapture. It is only those who do the will of God out of their desire to love God who shall be raptured before the great and terrible time of the tribulation. Scripture could not be any clearer for those who have ears to hear. And doesn't it make sense that when the "cream of the crop" is raptured from the face of the earth that there shall be nothing left to restrain the lawless one? When those who are Spirit filled; when those who are Spirit led; indeed, when those who are the faithful followers of Christ have been raptured, as is their lot adumbrated in the text of Second Thessalonians 2:7, then there will be no group of true believers left on earth.[6] Read the great words of Catherine Marshall in her book, *The Helper*.

> "In the new era [of the new testament], Jesus is telling us His glorified presence and His own resurrection life would be not only with us, but also in us (cf. John 16:7; 14:17), progressively to transform us and our lives, working from the inside outwardly. As the Apostle John would later describe it: *God's nature abides in him [us] . . . the divine sperm, remains permanently within him* (1 John 3:9, Amplified). This is the final outworking of that old testament promise: *I will put my law in their inward parts, and write it in their hearts . . .* (Jeremiah 31:33, KJV).
>
> "Here is a great mystery, difficult to put into words. It becomes real and practical to us only as we walk it out. Even in our time, we can observe two groups of Christians—those who have Christ beside them, *with* them, and those who have the Lord Jesus *in them*.

---

6. This is not entirely correct. As we shall see in chapter seven, the ministry of the two witnesses (Revelation 11:3-13) begins immediately upon the completion of the second rapture. During the period of the tribulation, these two specially anointed witnesses will at first be the sole mouthpieces of the Holy Spirit. At the onset of the tribulation, triggered as it will be by the second rapture, only these two witnesses will be filled with the Holy Spirit, and only these two true believers will remain in what will then become a truly non-Christian world.

"So many centuries ago, the prophet Ezekiel clearly foretold the two steps that must always take place before any one of us can have the ability to cope with the evil in our world and to possess power for service . . .

"The first step is a readying and cleansing process. 'A new spirit will I (God) put within you.' That is, God will, through the Spirit, renew and refresh our attitudes, convict us of sin, begin to teach us about obedience, change the thrust and climate of our inner beings. Thus He will be readying us for the crown and glory of His plan—that we, even in our flawed personhood, become the human temples of the Spirit. It was this cleansing and readying that the disciples had been experiencing during Jesus' earthly ministry and during the forty days and then the ten days they were waiting in Jerusalem prior to Pentecost.

"But many Christians, because they have never been told that there is something more than regeneration and this 'new spirit' within them, stop there. Among these are fine Bible students and church men and women active in the organizational work of their parish. Yet the excitement of the present-day, miracle-working Lord is missing because their eyes are still on what happened historically, back during Jesus' earthly ministry and in the early days of the Church. They have no concept of a contemporary Lord living *inside* them, the believers, working through them to redeem and heal others.

"The second necessary step was clearly foretold by Ezekiel, 'And I will put my Spirit *within* you.'" [7]

It is intended that the above section should portray only a glimpse of what is otherwise a rather complex theological issue regarding the Spirit-filled and Spirit-led Christian life. The nineteenth century religious philosopher William James was fond of affixing to true religious experiences the adverbial modifier, "ineffable," which simply means that words could never express such spiritually significant experiences even if one were to assiduously try. This important theological issue, then, of the Spirit-filled and Spirit-led Christian life, no doubt easily

---

7. Catherine Marshall, *The Helper* (New York: Chosen Books, a division of Baker Book House, ©1978), pp. 20-21, 26-27, emphases hers.

falls under such a rubric because it concerns itself with what appears to be the physical location of the Holy Spirit in the life of God's children. While this may sound absurd at first blush, it represents a serious attempt to understand a three-fold dilemma: One, Where is the Holy Spirit in the life of a heathen? And, Where is He in the life of what has otherwise been called a carnal Christian such that he is by definition not under the control and direction of the Holy Spirit? Two, How will new believers be drawn to Christ in the post-second rapture era without the presence of His Church which will have been theretofore His witness to all the nations? And then three, How will new believers in the post-second rapture get to heaven?

In what has been discussed above, it was hoped that an important theological distinction would be highlighted, namely, that the Spirit-filled and Spirit-led life seems to be mandated by Scripture in order for one to behold the assurance of salvation. So we must necessarily include a discussion of this aspect of the Christian life because the second rapture intimately ties itself to the removal of the Church as the vehicle of the Holy Spirit. John Wesley was fond of employing a term to refer to the work of the Holy Spirit in the lives of heathens to bring them to Christ. He called it "prevenient grace." Since most evangelical Christians believe that God through the Holy Spirit is actively working to bring all of His children to a saving faith in Him, we must nevertheless realize that many will not respond to Him, and thus they will be sentenced to eternal destruction.

So the issue of the physical location of the Holy Spirit as He works in a heathens life, as compared to the physical location of the Holy Spirit as He works in the life of a Spirit-filled and Spirit-led believer, becomes all the more controversial when we attempt to ascertain the location of the Holy Spirit in the life of a carnal or backsliden Christian. While thankful that there is no compunction to settle this issue in this work, it is nevertheless necessary to acknowledge it as it pertains to the removal of the Church at the second rapture.

Since many will be left behind after the second rapture, we can rest assured that those who are left behind did not, at the time of the second rapture, have the Holy Spirit inside of them, though all of them most certainly—through prevenient grace—had Him beside them, working to bring them to saving faith.

But who did not have the Holy Spirit inside of them? We can feel relatively at ease with saying that the heathen did not. And, conversely, we can say with the same sense of certainty that those who *ipso facto* were living the Spirit-led Christian life did.

But what about our carnal Christian friends who, as Catherine Marshall intimates, can be great pastors, scholars, and workers in the church? Obviously, in what was presented *supra*, scriptural references like Matthew 7:21-22 and Second Thessalonians 1:8 seem to confirm that the carnal Christian is to be considered in the same lot of eternal destination as the heathen. So all of this theological speculation about the Spirit-filled and Spirit-led Christian life takes on new meaning when we begin to imagine the world on earth after the second rapture has been executed: There will be a great many heathens left to run the world which remains after the upper torso Church has been raptured from it, but there will also be a great many carnal Christians left to mingle with what will appear to be their fellow heathen heirs of the tribulation. Hence the second horn of the triad dilemma: How will heathens and carnal Christians become true believers in the post-second rapture era without the presence of His upper torso Church which will have been theretofore His witness to the nations? How will heathens and carnal Christians in the post-second rapture era become members of the lower torso Church that will pay for its faith in Christ by being beheaded.[8]

How Some Will Become Christians After the Rapture of the Church

After the upper torso Church has been taken away in the second rapture, some who remain upon the earth will then realize the error of their ways and become true believers in Christ as God and Savior. In this book we are calling that period of time on earth, *the post-second rapture era*.[9] Christ's ascension was the first rapture, the birth of the

---

8. We have just introduced another new term, the *lower torso Church*. When the carnal Christian or heathen repents during the time of the tribulation, his repentance becomes the initiating act of membership in the lower torso Church.
9. As referred to in an earlier footnote, the *second rapture* is the same event as the *rapture of the upper torso Church*. It is identical to the *pretribulation rapture*.

head of the Church, the head of the image of King Nebuchadnezzar's dream. The upper torso Church's rapture in the near future will be the second rapture. (Obviously, then, such theological "jawboning" about the Spirit-filled life—as we have just done above—assumes an even more important dimension when we consider that there shall be multiple raptures to provide a population in heaven; a population which we have been calling throughout this book, the ruling, reigning body of Christ. Being Spirit-filled becomes *the* watershed event that separates the sheep from the goats.)

So there will be those who remain on earth after the upper torso Church is removed from the earth through the second rapture. Some of those who remain upon the earth will then become serious about spiritual matters of eternal importance. After having realized the mysterious disappearance of the upper torso Church, some of those left behind will thus come to the spiritually significant state of accepting the Holy Spirit to dwell *inside* of them, and no longer as merely a visitor *beside* them. It is the emergence of these new, fully devoted followers of the Lord Jesus that we now wish to augment by projecting ourselves into the future.

Imagine that the upper torso Church has just been raptured from the earth through the agency of what we are calling the second rapture. All (and we stress *all*) who were true believers in the Lord Jesus Christ would have been taken from the earth at that time.[10] At the instant the rapture of the upper torso Church was completed, *not one true believer remained on the earth*. At that moment—set into action by the awesomeness of what had just occurred—some would be spurred into rethinking their relationship with God. Broadly speaking—for the sake of communication—post-rapture conversions will emanate from two camps or types of people, namely, carnal Christians and heathens.[11]

Those most sensitive to the issue of their relationship with God (in the period of time after the rapture of the Church) would no doubt

---

10. See footnote six in this chapter for an important qualifier.
11. It is not significant that two types of people have been crudely divided. This was done simply to shed light upon the milieu of the post-second rapture era.

be the carnal Christians. Before the rapture of the upper torso Church, they may have answered to the name "Christian," though nominal as it may have been for them. (If it hasn't already been realized, part of the hypothesis contained in this work is that carnal Christians are not rapture-worthy.) But then, in the moments immediately following the rapture of the upper torso Church, some of these carnal Christians will realize the seriousness of the situation and rededicate themselves to the service of the Lord, thus becoming members of the lower torso Church.

Hence, this first group of post-rapture true believers will emerge from a group of carnal Christians who missed the rapture of the Church (the second rapture), *but had had a conversion experience some time before the rapture of the Church*. These will be the types found wanting in Matthew 7:21-22. These will be the types which today are claiming to be "born again" when in fact they are not *doing the will of God* as adjudicated in Second Thessalonians 1:8.

The mysterious occurrence of the rapture of the Church will stimulate in some of them a desire to enter a life of sincere devotion to the only wise God our Lord, the one alone who can save them. Having been found wanting at the time of the second rapture (the rapture of the upper torso Church), some of those who will be earthbound captives in the post-rapture era will repent and begin seriously living the Christian life. Theirs will then be a renewed but pensive devotion emanating from a newfound passion to serve Christ. Theirs will then be a recognition that the word of God was to be taken with sincerity and in truthfulness.

It is in these new-repentant, post-second rapture (but formerly carnal Christians) that the Holy Spirit will then take up His residence on earth to become the voice to those who will be living upon the earth in the wake of the rapture of the upper torso Church.[12] Theirs will be a ministry upon earth to the lost in the post-second rapture era.

From a second group—again, broadly speaking—will also emerge fully devoted followers of Jesus in a period of time we are calling the post-second rapture era. These new lower torso true believers will

---

12. See footnote six in this chapter for an important qualifier.

consist of those who had never before accepted Christ as personal Lord and Savior. Their conversions will come after the rapture of the upper torso Church, through the ministry of the Holy Spirit (through the ministry of the two witnesses to be discussed in chapter seven).

New believers will emerge from the pool of carnal Christians found wanting at the rapture of the upper torso Church; new believers also will emerge from the pool of God's creatures who had never before considered committing their lives to Him. Through the ministry of the Holy Spirit, carnal Christians will subsequently turn to a sincere devotion of Christ. And some who had never tasted the life of living in Christ will come to faith in Christ.

Each of these two groups, having beheld what will have just taken place, will turn to embrace Christ in deep sincerity.

The second horn of the dilemma, namely, *How shall post-second rapture inhabitants of earth come to saving faith in Christ without the presence of the witnessing Church?* has now been answered: The Holy Spirit's work will be at first through the lives of the two witnesses. It will also be through the lives of Christians who were found wanting at the time of the second rapture (which is why they missed the second rapture), but who subsequent to the second rapture began to take seriously the call of God upon their lives. Then, last of all, it will be through the witnessing of neophyte Christians, those who for the first time in their lives repented during the time of tribulation. Together these will become the voice of God to the spiritually lost, post-second rapture generation. We have but only the third and final horn of the dilemma to consider, namely, *How will these post-second rapture era true believers get to heaven?* [13]

From the subject matter presented in this chapter, it becomes obvious that some in the post-second rapture era will find Christ and then follow Him in sincerity and faithfulness. Immediately, then, one must reckon with the possibility of adding these new believers to the body of Christ which will have already been born in part (the head,

---

13. Appendix II contains a study of the meaning of *the second coming*. It may be worth your time reading this section now if you are unfamiliar with the important and significant nuances of its meaning.

the upper torso) through the agency of the first and the second raptures. Such a reckoning possesses the collateral effect of eventually confronting us with a compelling intellectual need to answer the question of the *means* of their salvation; the *means* of their being added to the body of Christ.

The means for the salvation of the souls of these neophyte and recommitted saints coming out of the post-second rapture era then, will also be through a process we are calling the rapture. Since the hypothesis contained herein posits the necessity of multiple rapture events for securing a population of saints in the ruling, reigning body of Christ it would therefore serve us well to examine the various rapture events which have not been discussed *in toto*. While the first rapture (the ascension of Christ) was presented in chapter four and the second rapture (the pre-tribulation rapture) was presented in chapter five, the next chapter concerns itself with the remaining three rapture events which are to take place during the period of the tribulation. Let us now look at the evidence for the succeeding raptures beyond the second rapture, to the third, the rapture of the tribulation saints.

7

How Will Tribulation Saints Get into Heaven?

When the Son of man comes in his glory, and all the Angels with him, then he will sit on his glorious throne. Before him will be gathered all the nations, and he will separate them one from another as a shepherd separates the sheep from the goats, and he will place the sheep at his right hand, but the goats at the left. Then the King will say to those at his right hand, "Come, O blessed of my Father, inherit the kingdom prepared for you from the foundation of the world; for I was hungry and you gave me food, I was thirsty and you gave me drink, I was a stranger and you welcomed me, I was naked and you clothed me, I was sick and you visited me, I was in prison and you came to me.

—Jesus of Nazareth (Matthew 25:31-40, RSV)

The Evidence of the Third Rapture

If it can be conceded that the second rapture is the event which eliminates the restraints of the son of perdition; and if it can be conceded that the second rapture removes from the face of the earth the Church of Spirit-filled believers; and if it can be conceded that the removal of the Church initiates the seven-year tribulation period; and if it can be conceded that after the second rapture the Holy Spirit will bring additional persons to true repentance on earth; then it must finally be conceded that God will have devised a plan to eventually induct them into the ruling, reigning body of heaven.

It has already been scripturally justified that a rapture will take place before the full revelation of the lawless one. This was shown to be the second rapture. But, in the premises just stated above, what was not shown to have been justified by Scripture is that after the second rapture there will be persons who will come to a sincere faith in our Lord Jesus Christ, who will be worthy of gaining placement in the ruling, reigning body. Since this becomes an important plank in the hypothesis of the rapture being an event which is more than once repeated, it is time to turn to the Holy Scriptures which show this to be the case.

In the first three chapters of the Book of Revelation, the Church is mentioned nineteen times as it existed on the earth. However, from the fourth through the nineteenth chapters of the Book of Revelation, there is not a single mention of the presence of the Church on earth. Interestingly enough, these chapters concern themselves with the descriptions of the horrifying details of the so-called time of Jacob's trouble (Jeremiah 30:7) alias the great tribulation (Matthew 24:21). So in the thirteenth chapter of the Book of Revelation, John the Revelator recounts this vision:

> *Then I saw another beast which rose out of the earth; it had two horns like a lamb and it spoke like a dragon. It exercises all the authority of the first beast in its presence, and makes the earth and its inhabitants worship the first beast, whose mortal wound was healed. It works great signs, even making fire come down from heaven to earth in the sight of men; and by the signs which it is allowed to work in the presence of the beast, it deceives those who dwell on life, bidding them make an image for the beast which was wounded by the sword and yet lived; and it was allowed to give breath to the image of the beast so that the image of the beast should even speak, and to cause those who would not worship the image of the beast to be slain* (Revelation 13:11-15, RSV).

We know that the beast does not make its appearance until "he who now restrains" him is taken out of the way (the Church in the second rapture). This text indicates that the beast will demand to be worshiped by all who will have been left behind in the wake of the second rapture. It also tells us of the horrifying means of the end of the lives of those who do not bow down to the Antichrist: they shall be slain. (This is an important point, which will be invoked anon.) Now it is possible—from just reading this text alone—that Revelation 13:15 may represent a hard-core group of secular rebels who, having no faith in God whatsoever, will find it more appealing to die a horrible death than to serve in submissive servanthood to what they perceive to be a prodigiously arrogant dictator. And we can grant that this is entirely possible and most certainly will occur. Indeed, this text *per se* does not indicate that true believers are the ones who refuse to worship the image of the beast. But the next chapter of the Book of Revelation does:

And another angel, a third, followed them, saying with a loud voice, "If any one worships the beast and its image, and receives a mark on his forehead or on his hand, he also shall drink the wine of God's wrath, poured unmixed into the cup of his anger, and he shall be tormented with fire and sulfur in the presence of the holy angels and in the presence of the Lamb. And the smoke of their torment goes up for ever and ever; and they have no rest, day or night, these worshipers of the beast and its image, and whoever receives the mark of its name." Here is a call for the endurance of the saints, those who keep the commandments of God and the faith of Jesus. And I heard a voice from heaven saying, "Write this: Blessed are the dead who die in the Lord henceforth." "Blessed indeed," says the Spirit, "that they may rest from their labors, for their deeds follow them!" Then I looked, and lo, a white cloud, and seated on the cloud one like a son of man, with a golden crown on his head, and a sharp sickle in his hand. And another angel came out of the temple, calling with a loud voice to him who sat upon the cloud, "Put in your sickle, and reap, for the hour to reap has come, for the harvest of the earth is fully ripe." So he who sat upon the cloud swung his sickle on the earth, and the earth was reaped (Revelation 14:9-16, RSV).

The "hour to reap" is the salvation of the then believers in the post-second rapture era; it is a rapture event which will occur during the period of the tribulation, a tribulation which is initiated after the second rapture will have been executed. This reaping, however, carries with it an intriguing implication: Those Christian believers who come to new faith in Christ during the period of the tribulation will not only be martyred but, upon their death, they will be temporarily held in what appears to be a unique sub-section of heaven:

When he [the Lamb] opened the fifth seal, I saw under the altar the souls of those who had been slain for the word of God and for the witness they had borne; they cried out with a loud voice, "O Sovereign Lord, holy and true, how long before thou wilt judge and avenge our blood on those who dwell upon the earth?" Then they were each given a white robe and told to rest a little longer, until the number of their fellow servants and their brethren should be complete, who were to be killed as they themselves had been (Revelation 6:9-11, RSV).

While not every nuance of each rapture event is provided to sufficiently answer all of the questions emanating from our intellectual curiosity, the following details can be ascertained.

The third rapture (the reaping) will be a unique rapture. It will be a rapture only for those who have reconstituted their faith during the period of the tribulation. It will occur as a separate event in the eschatological parade. In this divinely sanctioned parade, those who have already been raptured, plus the myriad of other heavenly hosts of angels, will witness the induction of this special group of believers into the ruling, reigning body of Christ. It is almost as though God's plan, like the order of the procession in any parade, will be to announce to a cheering body the special status of the next wave of Saints to be raptured, to be added to the ruling, reigning body of Christ: Those who paid for their faith in Christ with the shedding of their own blood.

Now the second unique characteristic of the third rapture is that there seems to be a kind of holding tank in heaven for these martyred, tribulation saints: It is under the altar in heaven. This abode contains those who will have been slain during the period of the tribulation on account of their faith in Christ. This abode will become their temporary, post-death domicile. Once the full number has been achieved of those who will ever die as a result of their faithfulness during the period of the tribulation, it is then, as a unit together, that they shall achieve the full privileged liberty already granted their fellow heirs in heaven. In the text just quoted, the full number of martyred saints has not been reached. And in this text, they are in conversation with God: Whatever the complexities of the process of the Divine Order (which are not at our disposal to understand), these saints are detained in heaven under the altar of the Most High God. It can only be assumed, therefore, that they have not yet achieved the full privileges associated with being part of the ruling, reigning body of Christ.[1]

Nevertheless, Revelation 6:9-11 clinches the argument for a mid-tribulation rapture: since the "saints under the altar" are in direct conversation with God, we know that they are already in heaven; and since they are given the white robes of heaven; and since they are told to wait for their other "brethren" to be slain; and since we know that during the tribulation those who do not worship the Antichrist will be slain; then the rapture of the slain saints during the tribulation becomes an incontrovertible fact. The fate, then, of those saints who did not bow down to the beast or its image during the period of the tribulation is recalled by John the Revelator in the twentieth chapter:

> *Then I saw thrones, and seated on them were those to whom judgment was committed. Also I saw the souls of those who had been beheaded for their testimony to Jesus and for the word of God, and who had not worshiped the beast or its image only and had not received its mark on their foreheads or their hands. They came to life, and reigned with Christ a thousand years* (Revelation 20:4, RSV).

From these scriptural principles, it can be seen that there shall be a group of Christians (in the true sense of the word) who will have reconstituted their faith in Christ after the second rapture. It can also be seen that the "reaping of the harvest" is the plucking of these tribulation saints from the poisonous pool of persecution under the revealed presence of the man acting in the capacity of the lawless one. Their "plucking" will not be like that of the living saints during the second rapture: All tribulation saints, according to the Scriptures, will be slain. There will be none alive to benefit from a living rapture like will be possible during the second rapture. Upon their death, they

---

1. Regardless of these unique characteristics, of which this latter one titillates the curiosity more so than the other, it was not intended for us to now understand. As alluded to in chapter three under footnote eight, there are some things which God chooses not to reveal to us, and thus keeps it as His secret. See especially Deuteronomy 29:29.

shall be immediately placed in the eternal security of the domiciliary of heaven, albeit a unique part of heaven, until the full number of martyred saints is achieved.

We mentioned earlier, in referring to Revelation 13:11-15, that we would return to an important point concerning the fate of those who would come to know Christ in the post-second rapture era. The death of the martyred saints is important because of the unique absence of a specific rapture event recorded during the time of the tribulation period. It may have gone unnoticed that no particular reference to the time of the occurrence of the third rapture was established. Both the first and the second raptures were clearly punctilious events, representing clearly distinct occurrences identified by scriptural references. Such is not the case for the third rapture. We know that there shall be post-second rapture conversions to Christ. And we know that these tribulation saints will get into the ruling, reigning body of Christ. What is absent from the Scriptures is a specific instance of a single rapture event for the martyred saints. Furthermore, the texts quoted about the fate of the post-second rapture saints tell us that all who do not worship the beast, and all who refuse to have "the mark" put upon their bodies shall be slain. Which means that none of them could be alive to be raptured as those in the second rapture were. It also means that the third rapture is an event which will span the first three-and-a-half years of a seven-year tribulation period. (The three-and-a-half year period will be explained in the next chapter.) As each saint is slain during the period of the tribulation, his soul will be added into the domiciliary of the under region of the altar of heaven, to be held there until the full number of their fraternal martyred comrades will be added to the same.

It may be tempting to sense a note of poetic justice in all of this, but too dangerous to succumb. That is, while the scriptural principles to the validity of the work of God to bring His people to salvation will have been rather axiomatic up until the time of the second rapture, it will be after this event, for anyone who possesses even a semblance of spiritual sensibility, that the accounts predicted in the Holy Scriptures shall certainly take place. Indeed, even for those of us now living in this pretribulation era who are more concerned about other things than finding and doing the will of God, who may survive the second rapture to find themselves living in the world of the revealed Antichrist: What better sense of justice could be meted out to those who have toed the line to faithful and obedient Christian living but have failed to actually do so? Since the evidence of the validity of the Scriptures concerning the reality of Christ will increase an indeterminate amount on earth after the second rapture, so will the persecution on earth increase an indeterminate amount against those who *posthaste* attempt to be faithful followers of the Lord Jesus Christ after the second rapture. Indeed, the increase in the rate and severity of persecution in the post-second rapture era will be indicated by the payment of their faith by death. Not a one shall be raptured alive. But then, we are thankful not to have to play God. We are thankful that in His infinite wisdom the issues of life and death are in His divine balances, and not human ones.

So the first rapture was the ascension of Christ. The second rapture will be the pretribulation saints whose catching away will immediately incite the events which will lead to the full disclosure of the son of perdition in the service of Satan. And the third rapture will be the tribulation saints who *post de facto* the second rapture come to genuine faith in Christ. But the third rapture will not be a punctilious event like the first and the second raptures because there will be no living Christians. They shall all be slain.

In spite of what seems to be an inclusive third rapture of all martyred saints during the period of the tribulation, scriptural evidence indicates that there shall be yet another rapture during the first half of the seven-year stretch known as the time of Jacob's trouble.

The Fourth Rapture

While it has just been established that the third rapture will not be a punctilious event like the first and the second raptures, the fourth rapture is quickly indited under this charge as well. We are certain of the time of the first rapture, it being the case *de facto*. And of the time of the second rapture we can amass some detail of the general time of its occurrence. When it comes to the third and the fourth raptures, we are constrained to delimit the occurrence of both to a period of time of three-and-a-half years after the second rapture.

This three-and-a-half-year time period is the first half of the tribula-tion period.[2] We are not as yet, however, able to ascertain by scriptur-al injunction which should occur first: the third or the fourth rapture. So, before we turn to the scriptural justification for an additional rapture event during the period of the tribulation, it must be under-stood that the chronological sequence of the third and the fourth raptures cannot be determined conclusively from Scripture—just that they do occur as two separate events, or like two aspects of the same rapture.[3] While the ancient writers of the word of God no doubt felt intellectually comfortable with ambiguity, the Western-rationalistic mind senses a need to rid the world of the same. So we attempt to strap onto Scripture a Western-rationalistic thought process which dictates that Scripture ought to adhere to a rather linear progression of events when in fact they do not always. But, as is especially common in the literature of the Bible, sequences of events as recorded

---

2. While the full evidence for this will be covered under the fifth rapture *infra*, let it simply be said for now that the fifth rapture is justified by Scripture to take place during the exact midpoint of the seven-year tribula-tion. Therefore, the third and the fourth raptures must occur sometime between the start of the time of the tribulation and the midpoint of the same, a three-and-one-half-year period. Chapter nine will deal with the subject matter of the timing of the tribulation.

3. The employment of this simile is an attempt to portray a more fluid movement of an event we are calling the birth of the Manchild *von* the rapture. As in the normal birth of any child, once the shoulders have penetrated the outside world, the rest of the body not only appears rapid-ly, but it occurs in a continuous, smooth, and uninterrupted fashion. It is also interesting that the timeline of the entire birth of the Manchild is akin to the birth of any child: The head often appears suspended in motion protruding from the opening of the birth canal as its shoulders await its advent. This is the birth of the head of the Manchild, Christ. Once the shoulders appear, the rest of the body quickly passes through the birth canal. It has been nearly two millennia since the head was born, but once the arms and breast of the Manchild are born (the second rapture), it is only three-and-a-half years before the entire body of the Manchild is born. So to talk about the birth of the child's torso, as opposed to his belly, is not really to talk about two separate events, but different aspects of the birth. We are not talking about mutually exclusive events, but different aspects of the process of the birth of the ruling, reigning body of Christ.

particularly in the prophetic sections of the Holy Bible do not follow a logical progression of chronologically ordered events. Indeed, the Book of Revelation may be the paragon of this literary, biblical style: the Book of Revelation continually cycles a chronological time period; it jumps back and forth between time periods as easily as it ends one sentence with a period and begins the next. It is therefore incumbent upon journeyman hermeneutical students to suspend the *fait accompli* of Western rationalism to see that the pieces of the puzzle we are calling the mystery of God are strewn throughout the Book of Revelation in no necessary logical progression of chronologically ordered events.

An epitome of this suspension is the realization that the chronological sequence of the third and the fourth raptures cannot be determined conclusively from the scant scriptural references about them. So they are simply listed as the third and the fourth almost by random choice. Having done so, however, does not in anyway detract from the evidence which Scripture demands for the third and the fourth rapture events indicated to occur during the time of tribulation. So let us then turn to the evidence for the occurrence of the fourth rapture event.

Scriptural Evidence of the Fourth Rapture

Then I saw another angel ascend from the rising of the sun, with the seal of the living God, and he called with a loud voice to the four angels who had been given power to harm earth and sea, saying, "Do not harm the earth or the sea or the trees, till we have sealed the servants of our God upon their foreheads." And I heard the number of the sealed, a hundred and forty-four thousand sealed, out of every tribe of the sons of Israel, twelve thousand sealed out of the tribe of Judah, twelve thousand of the tribe of Reuben, twelve thousand of the tribe of Gad, twelve thousand of the tribe of Asher, twelve thousand of the tribe of Naph'tali, twelve thousand of the tribe of Manas'seh, twelve thousand of the tribe of Simeon, twelve thousand of the tribe of Levi, twelve thousand of the tribe of Is'sachar, twelve thousand of the tribe of Zeb'ulun, twelve thousand of the tribe of Joseph, twelve thousand sealed out of the tribe of Benjamin (Revelation 7:2-8, RSV).

This portion of Scripture indisputably decrees non-Gentile Jews. It unmistakably specifies that a select group of Jews will be marked for the Manchild birthing process during the time of the tribulation. The seventh chapter of the Book of Revelation, out of which this passage is taken, is an interlude between John's vision of the sixth seal and his vision of the seventh seal. The fifth seal (Revelation 6:9-11) concerns itself with the first of the martyrs of the tribulation who are kept under the altar. The sixth seal (Revelation 6:12-17) spells out the beginning of the pouring out of God's wrath. It is in this context that the above-quoted scriptural passage (Revelation 7:2-8) takes place: The angels who are to blow the trumpets of judgment upon nonbelievers are instructed to withhold their wind until the Jews numbering a hundred and forty-four thousand can be raptured from the face of an increasingly violent earth. The seventh seal which follows this interlude, then, is the solemn though ominous half hour of heavenly silence before the trumpets of judgment are blown. We learn the fate of the one hundred and forty-four thousand in the first verses of chapter fourteen, which show this multitude already in heaven:

Then I looked, and lo, on Mount Zion stood the Lamb, and with him a hundred and forty-four thousand who had his name and his Father's name written on their foreheads. And I heard a voice from heaven like the sound of many waters and like the sound of loud thunder; the voice I heard was like the sound of harpers playing on their harps, and they sing a new song before the throne and before the four living creatures and before the elders. No one could learn that song except the hundred and forty-four thousand who had been redeemed from the earth. It is these who have not defiled themselves with women, for they are chaste; it is these who follow the Lamb wherever he goes; these have been redeemed from mankind as first fruits for God and the Lamb, and in their mouth no lie was found, for they are spotless (Revelation 14:1-5, RSV).

The one hundred and forty-four thousand who will be redeemed from the population of people left upon earth during the time of tribulation will be the Jews who "follow the Lamb wherever He goes." Their reward shall be eternal life in heaven, and membership in the ruling, reigning body of Christ. And while it is not clear which rapture the third or the fourth shall precede the other, it is certain from an investigation of the Scriptures that each represents a separate event which is to take place during the time of the tribulation. We have but one final rapture event which is enjoined by Scripture: the fifth rapture.

Fifth Rapture

Earlier in this work it was said that in the conventional wisdom and usage of the scholars in the field of apocalyptic eschatology, the rapture refers to that eschatological event wherein believers will be "snatched up" from the earth in a process which incorporates them as permanent members of the ruling, reigning body of Christ. It was said that no quibbling or caviling should take place with this innocent parochial usage of the term. Rather, it was said that this work intended to establish that the rapture, being duly subsumed in this work under the rubric of "the birth," shall be an event which is more than once executed. Thus far Scripture has adjudicated four clearly distinguishable rapture events. But there is one final rapture associated with the birth of the Manchild. It is the rapture of the two witnesses. The final rapture of the saints of God.

In chapter two, it was intended therein to establish the presence of an adumbration in the Book of Daniel which pointed to the concept of the Manchild in the Book of Revelation. In so doing, two examples of parallel passages of Scripture were invoked which concerned themselves with similar visions (Ezekiel and the eating of the scrolls; Zechariah and the two lamp stands). In each of these cases, a passage out of Revelation was cited along with the passage out of the Old Testament. One of those comparisons was, as you will remember, John the Revelator's vision of the two witnesses which the Prophet Zechariah had also been given. In that comparison it was said that it was only coincidental that the subject matter of that example was also integral to the theory of the Manchild. It was said that the example of the two witnesses who will be slain and left in the streets unburied (Revelation 11:3-12) would be discussed in much fuller detail at the end of another chapter, where its unique meaning and significance would be given as it specifically relates to the concept of the Manchild. It is now time to do this.

In the eleventh chapter of the Book of Revelation, the future history is given of the ministry of the two witnesses who will live during the time of the tribulation. The eleventh chapter of the Book of Revelation falls under the blowing of the sixth trumpet of judgment upon nonbelievers, just before the blowing of the seventh and final trumpet blowing which will usher in the birth of the Manchild as the ruling, reigning body of the promised kingdom of God. But the eleventh chapter of the Book of Revelation follows the third and the fourth raptures in Revelation of chapter seven. So, after the third and the fourth raptures, but just before the birth of the Manchild in the first verses of chapter twelve, there comes the story of the two witnesses in chapter eleven:

> *"I will grant my two witnesses power to prophesy for one thousand two hundred and sixty days, clothed in sackcloth." These are the two olive trees and the two lampstands which stand before the Lord of the earth. And if any one would harm them, fire pours out from their mouth and consumes their foes; if any one would harm them, thus he is doomed to be killed. They have power to shut the sky, that no rain may fall during the days of their prophesying, and they have power over the waters to turn them into blood, and to smite the earth with every plague, as often as they desire. And when they have finished their testimony, the beast that ascends from the bottomless pit will make war upon them and conquer them and kill them, and their dead bodies will lie in the street of the great city which is allegorically called Sodom and Egypt, where their Lord was crucified. For three days and a half men from the peoples and tribes and tongues and nations gaze at their dead bodies and refuse to let them be placed in a tomb, and those who dwell on the earth will rejoice over them and make merry and exchange presents, because these two prophets had been a torment to those who dwell on the earth. But after the three and a half days a breath of life from God entered them, and they stood up on their feet, and great fear fell on those who saw them. Then they heard a loud voice from heaven saying to them, "Come up hither!" And in the sight of their foes they went up to heaven in a cloud. And at that hour there was a great earthquake, and a tenth of the city fell; seven thousand people were killed in the earthquake, and the rest were terrified and gave glory to the God of heaven* (Revelation 11:3-13, RSV).

While all of the other tribulation saints shall be caught up into heaven in one of two raptures, the two witnesses will not benefit from either. The duration of their ministry is given as one thousand two hundred and sixty days (vs. 3). This is exactly three-and-one-half years, which means that it must start at the onset of the tribulation[4] initiated by the second rapture, which, as we have already established, is the rapture of the upper torso Church.[5] Furthermore, the implication of this established length of time of ministry for the two witnesses bids that the two witnesses will not only live past the time of the third rapture of the lower torso Saints, but also past the fourth rapture of the one hundred and forty-four thousand who represent the legs of the Manchild. Indeed, since their prophetic ministry begins when the second rapture is an accomplished fact, we can hold some confidence that those who come to genuine faith in Christ during the tribulation will do so as a result of their ministry. But what a ministry! These two witnesses must live in the period of the tribulation knowing that they are especially anointed to survive the third and the fourth raptures. Indeed, they most certainly will know that according to the Holy Scriptures they must be slain near the midpoint of the tribulation which shall be accompanied by a surmounting hideous evil. They will be very special witnesses. So let's take a look at the identity of these two saints.

---

4. While the appearance of these two prophets will no doubt be an astounding event, we can but only speculate as to the means of their return. While the intent of this work does not include such conjecture, one thing can be stated with some certainty: that a dumfounded world living in the wake of the supernatural event of the second rapture will indeed be stunned. The world will no doubt want to believe in anything, which is one reason it will eventually worship the Antichrist.
5. Although it has now been said a number of times that we will deal with this timetable in another chapter, we must again defer the discussion of the tribulation to the next chapter, where we will attempt to draw together all of the loose strings of the pieces associated with the timing of the tribulation that have been posited in various places throughout this work.

Two phrases have become Christian idioms which must be distinguished. The first of these is "the day of Christ," which is concerned with the glorification of the saints through their rapture, and their reward in the heavenly realm. "The day of Christ" is therefore to be taken as synonymous with the birth of the Manchild as the ruling, reigning body of Christ. But "the day of Christ" is not to be taken as synonymous with the second phrase requiring discernment, namely, "the day of the Lord."

The phrase "the day of the Lord" occurs twenty-three times throughout the entire Bible. Like the phrase "the second coming," the phrase "the day of the Lord" depends upon which camp one emerges when he begins to interpret it. In general, however, "the day of the Lord" refers to that protracted period of time ostensibly commencing with the second advent of our Lord in His glory to mete out justice and vengeance upon humanity, but ending with the cleansing of the heavens and the earth by fire in preparation for eternity. The concept of the Manchild necessitates a fine tuning of certain nuances. So, while the phrase "the day of the Lord" possesses some deficiency of definition, it may be worthwhile to portray its meaning in terms cognate with the thesis of this work.

"The day of the Lord" encompasses a string of events. It begins with "the day of Christ," alias the birth of the Manchild as the ruling, reigning body of Christ. This event will be the one which will inaugurate "the day of the Lord." But, as we have been saying, the birth of the Manchild is completed at the midpoint of the tribulation. Obviously, then, after the birth of the ruling, reigning body Christ, three-and-one-half years will remain (the last half of the tribulation period) for unredeemed humanity to live out their lives over the face of the earth. The seven-year tribulation period will end, however, with the return of the ruling, reigning body of Christ to mete out punishment and judgment upon the earth in the mother of all battles, the Battle of Armageddon. The return of the ruling, reigning body of Christ will be a ubiquitous physical manifestation over the face of the earth at the end of the seven-year tribulation period. "The day of the Lord" comprehends not only the closing phase of the period of the seven-year tribulation, it extends through the millennial kingdom which is ushered in by the second advent of Christ alias the return of the Manchild as the ruling, reigning body of Christ.

So, in the terminology of the thesis presented in this work, "the day of the Lord" commences with the birth of the Manchild as the ruling, reigning body of Christ, continues on through the last half of the tribulation, encompasses the return of the ruling, reigning body of Christ as it doles out retribution upon the remaining inhabitants of earth, perseveres with the restoration of God's earth in preparation for eternity, and persists through the millennial reign of the ruling, reigning body of Christ.

However, before the return of the ruling, reigning body of Christ as the second advent, the Manchild as the ruling, reigning body of Christ must be born. This birth, of course, is the birth of the Manchild. This birth, as we have just noted, inaugurates "the day of the Lord." But this birth cannot occur until certain scriptural prophecies are fulfilled. Of particular interest to the timetable of "the day of the Lord" as apocalyptic realization is the prophet Malachi who prophesies that God *will send you Elijah the prophet before the coming of the great and dreadful day of the LORD* (Malachi 4:5, KJV).

Jesus identified John the Baptist's coming as a preliminary fulfillment of this prophecy in Matthew 11:14. But the coming of John the Baptist was merely a prototype. He was not Elijah.[6] Elijah has yet to come in physical form in fulfillment of the words spoken by the prophet Malachi. So Elijah must yet come in order to fulfill the

---

6. John the Baptist repeatedly denied that he was Elijah (John 1:21,25). While Elijah was present at the transfiguration of Jesus in Matthew 17:1-5, he did not come to his people as Malachi predicted, but was merely visible for this spiritually significant event. The closest thing we have to John the Baptist being identified as Elijah is Matthew 17:10-12, where Jesus, using a mixture of future and present tenses, conveys what may otherwise be a confusing message for one "who does not have ears." Jesus clearly spoke of an eschatological task (hence His use of the future tense) that Elijah had not yet fulfilled, relating it to His second coming. But He also related John the Baptist's fulfilled task (of announcing His first coming) to Elijah: Jesus referred to John the Baptist as having come in the spirit and power of Elijah to do before the first advent what Elijah will yet do before the second advent.

prophecy of God. We do not possess the option of simply spiritualizing the words of Malachi. Indeed, we could easily allegorize the prophecy of Malachi if it were not for one of the more interesting aspects of Elijah's life which is recorded in the following Scripture reference:

When the LORD was about to take Elijah up to heaven in a whirlwind, Elijah and Elisha were on their way from Gilgal. The company of the prophets at Bethel came out to Elisha and asked, "Do you know that the LORD is going to take your master from you today?" "Yes, I know," Elisha replied, "but do not speak of it." When they had crossed, Elijah said to Elisha, "Tell me, what can I do for you before I am taken from you?" "Let me inherit a double portion of your spirit," Elisha replied. "You have asked a difficult thing," Elijah said, "yet if you see me when I am taken from you, it will be yours—otherwise not." As they were walking along and talking together, suddenly a chariot of fire and horses of fire appeared and separated the two of them, and Elijah went up to heaven in a whirlwind. Elisha saw this and cried out, "My father! My father! The chariots and horsemen of Israel!" And Elisha saw him no more (2 Kings 2:1,3,9-12, NIV).

Elijah holds a special place in the life of God's people as one who did not die, but was taken up directly to heaven without first dying. There is only one other recorded subject in this unique class of human being: Enoch.

Enoch was the son of Jared (Genesis 5:18) and the father of the legendary Methuselah (Genesis 5:21). In the next three verses we learn of his unique destiny in the history of the saints of God: *Enoch walked with God after the birth of Methu'selah three hundred years, and had other sons and daughters. Thus all the days of Enoch were three hundred and sixty-five years. Enoch walked with God; and he was not, for God took him* (Genesis 5:22-24, RSV). The Book of Hebrews confirms this astounding occurrence: *By faith Enoch was taken up so that he should not see death; and he was not found, because God had taken him. Now before he was taken he was attested as having pleased God* (11: 5).

As a reward for their holiness, both Elijah and Enoch were transported directly into heaven without the casualty of death. A little earlier in the Book of Hebrews, another astounding pontification is made: *It is appointed for men to die once, and after that comes judgment* (9:27, RSV). Have Elijah and Enoch died? Indeed not. Shall they indeed die? Only if Scripture does not lie.

According to Malachi, Elijah will be coming back before *the day of the Lord*. "The day of the Lord," however, is inaugurated with the birth of the Manchild as the ruling, reigning body of Christ. So then we know that Elijah must return before this time. But, as we have already established, the rapture of the two witnesses enjoins the birth of the Manchild. Furthermore, we have already established that the duration of the ministry of the two witnesses commences with the second rapture, and duly ends with their rapture at the midpoint of the tribulation. So we are led to the incontrovertible conclusion that the two witnesses are Elijah and Enoch who must fulfill their appointment "to die once." Because they were faithful as they walked over the face of this earth, God will bring them back at the vacation of the upper torso Church via the second rapture. Their special and unique ministry will last three-and-a-half years. Since it is appointed for men to die but once, they will be slain according to the Scriptures. When they are resurrected; when they are raptured, these two witnesses will represent the feet of the Manchild. Their rapture, their birth, will render the birthing process final. The Manchild will then be born. The ruling, reigning body of Christ shall be completed. All who would ever come to saving faith in Christ will be completed. The door to eternal life will be shut. The fifth rapture, consisting of the two witnesses alias "the two feet" of the Manchild, completes the birth of the ruling, reigning body of Christ.

8

More on the Tribulation

Seventy weeks of years are decreed concerning your people and your holy city to finish the transgression, to put an end to sin, and to atone for iniquity, to bring in everlasting righteousness, to seal both vision and prophet, and to anoint a most holy place. Know therefore and understand that from the going forth of the word to restore and build Jerusalem to the coming of an anointed one, a prince, there shall be seven weeks. Then for sixty-two weeks it shall be built again with squares and moat, but in a troubled time. And after the sixty-two weeks, an anointed One shall be cut off, and shall have nothing; and the people of the prince who is to come shall destroy the city and the sanctuary. Its end shall come with a flood, and to the end there shall be war; desolations are decreed. And he shall make a strong covenant with many for one week; and for half of the week he shall cause sacrifice and offering to cease; and upon the wing of abominations shall come one who makes desolate, until the decreed end is poured out on the desolator.

—The Jewish Prophet Daniel (Daniel 9:24-29, RSV)

While the preceding Scripture reference has been the object of study by myriad scholars, this work will not reckon with the enormous scholastic work already done on it. It is therefore not the scope of this book to initiate an exegetical study of this pericope from the Book of Daniel. Rather it is to build upon the conclusions derived from those academic giants who have labored before us. Hence, while it may not become readily apparent to the neophyte student of biblical, apocalyptic literature that Daniel is here predicting the seven-year tribulation, conventional scholarly wisdom suggests that the seventieth week of Daniel represents the last seven years of human history as we know it. The seventieth week of Daniel represents the seven-year tribulation made notorious by John the Revelator in the Book of Revelation. This last period of time in the history of the world as we shall know it has been called "the time of Jacob's trouble," and "the great tribulation." But, as seems to be the common lot in this field of apocalyptic eschatology, there is some uncertainty attached to the employment of these phrases.

The exact phrase, "the great tribulation," is found only once throughout the entire Bible. It is found in the Book of Revelation:

> *Then one of the elders addressed me, saying, "Who are these, clothed in white robes, and whence have they come?" I said to him, "Sir, you know." And he said to me, "These are they who have come out of the great tribulation; they have washed their robes and made them white in the blood of the Lamb"* (Revelation 7:13-14, RSV).

Once again, on account of the Scriptures being practically reticent concerning its exact meaning, there is a diversity of opinion about the timing of the great tribulation: Is it referring to the first half of the seven-year tribulation period? Or is it referring to the latter half of the same? Some scholars suggest that the first half of the seven-year tribulation period ought to be to called the lesser tribulation, while the second half should be referred to as the great tribulation. Regardless of this minor theological consideration, the argument is nevertheless restricted to an occurrence during the seven-year period known as the seventieth week of Daniel, the final seven-year future history of the world. (The Scriptures also speak of a general tribulation which all believers experience [Matthew 13:21; John 16:33; Acts 14:22]. But this has nothing to do with the seventieth week of Daniel.) By putting the differences of nuance contained in these distinctions into the theological crucible, the following parameters receive general consensus by the varying camps of theological persuasion: 1) Daniel's seventieth week is the seven-year tribulation; 2) the seven-year tribulation period will be characterized by a rapid rise and revelation of the son of perdition, the lawless one, who will be in service of Satan himself; 3) the seven-year tribulation period will consist of two parts, the first and second halves; while both will be terrible, the second half will be even more terrible than the world has ever known; 4) the seven-year tribulation period will be the last period of time which will represent the close of this present age; 5) the seven-year tribulation period will end with a coming of the Lord Jesus and His body.

When the force which is now restraining the liberty of the Anti-christ is taken out of the way viz. the removal of the upper torso Church in the second rapture, second Thessalonians 2:1-9 states that this event will thereby signal the first day of what the prophets have been predicting and calling the time of Jacob's trouble, otherwise known as the seven-year period of tribulation. While the various distinctions about the terminology are not critical to the thesis of this work, it would be safe to refer to the last seven years of human his-tory as we know it to: the time of Jacob's trouble; the seven-year tribulation period; the seventieth week of Daniel; and, loosely, the great tribulation.[1]

What is of particular interest to this work is the timing of the rapture events during the seven-year period of the tribulation, which will be executed to secure a group of faithful believers to serve as the ruling, reigning body of Christ in eternity. In Revelation 11:3, which was quoted *supra*, God said that He *will grant my two witnesses power to prophesy for one thousand two hundred and sixty days* (RSV). This number of days is exactly three-and-one-half years. The next account in the Book of Revelation, occurring after the rapture of the two witnesses, is the passage regarding the birth of the Manchild:

---

1. It would become quibbling to dwell longer on this minor theological consideration. However, as a footnote in the hypothesis of this book, it should be noted that the term "the great tribulation" in Revelation 7:13-14 expressly refers to the martyred saints. Since, according to the theory promulgated in this work, there will be no conversions to Christ after the rapture of the two witnesses, and since the rapture of the two witnesses comes at the midpoint of the tribulation, we are led to the incontrovert-ible conclusion that the only usage of the term "the great tribulation" must refer to the first half of the tribulation period. However, this theo-logical distinction carries with it no significant ramification.

And there appeared a great wonder in heaven; the woman clothed with the sun, and the moon under her feet, and upon her head a crown of twelve stars: And she being with child cried, travailing in birth, and pained to be delivered. And there appeared another wonder in heaven; and behold a great red dragon, having seven heads and ten horns, and seven crowns upon his heads. And his tail drew the third part of the stars of heaven, and did cast them to the earth: and the dragon stood before the woman which was ready to be delivered, for to devour her child as soon as it was born. And she brought forth a Manchild, who was to rule all nations with a rod of iron: and her child was caught up unto God, and to his throne (Revelation 12:1-5, RSV).

Then, after the Manchild has been given birth; after the ruling, reigning body of Christ has been established and sealed for eternal security and salvation, the next account in the Book of Revelation concerns itself with the rise of the beast from the sea; the unmitigated rise of power of the Antichrist. And in this next account in the Book of Revelation, John the Revelator sets the chronological limit of the Antichrist's reign on earth: *And the beast was given a mouth uttering haughty and blasphemous words, and it was allowed to exercise authority for forty-two months* (Revelation 13:5, RSV).

Forty-two months also equals three-and-one-half years. So while the last two faithful witnesses of God walk over the face of the earth (in the personages of the two witnesses), their power and might will represent the last vestiges of restraint over the Antichrist. When the two witnesses are raptured, after three-and-one-half years, there is nothing on earth left to resist the Antichrist. This final epoch in the history of man, as we know it, lasts only seven years. If the two witnesses evangelize during the first half of the seven-year tribulation period, then the Antichrist's reign of power must be the second half of the tribulation period. Which is no doubt the reason the second half of the tribulation period is sometimes referred to as the great period of tribulation: There will be no faithful witnesses of God left on earth; indeed, there shall never be any during this period. The Antichrist will possess an absolute reign of power.

Knowing that the two witnesses will remain for the first half of the tribulation period, we know that the rule of the Antichrist can last only three-and-one-half years because the tribulation period lasts only seven years. So his reign must necessarily last three-and-one-half years, ending when Christ with His body alias the ruling, reigning body of Christ pay reverent attendance upon the face of the earth to destroy the Antichrist and those who worship him in the Battle of Armageddon. Knowing the ministry of the two witnesses spans the first half of the tribulation period, this necessarily means that the rapture *in toto* (i.e., the five rapture events comprising the entire birth of the Manchild) will be completed not only when the two witnesses have been raptured, but at the exact midpoint of the tribulation period.

While the contents of this short chapter merely represent a summary of the various references to the period of the tribulation sprinkled throughout this work, it was nevertheless necessary to tie them together in one chapter. What remains for the duration of this work is the exploitation of the relationship between the adumbration of the Manchild whose genesis is found in King Nebuchadnezzar's dream, and the vision of the Manchild as given to John the Revelator. This last piece of the apocalyptic puzzle is appropriately called the denouement.

9

Putting All the Pieces Together

You saw, O king, and behold, a great image. This image, mighty and of exceeding brightness, stood before you, and its appearance was frightening. The head of this image was of fine gold, its breast and arms of silver, its belly and thighs of bronze, its legs of iron, its feet partly of iron and partly of clay. As you looked, a stone was cut out by no human hand, and it smote the image on its feet of iron and clay, and broke them in pieces; then the iron, the clay, the bronze, the silver, and the gold, all together were broken in pieces, and became like the chaff of the summer threshing floors; and the wind carried them away, so that not a trace of them could be found. But the stone that struck the image became a great mountain and filled the whole earth. The God of heaven will set up a kingdom which shall never be destroyed, nor shall its sovereignty be left to another people, and it shall stand forever.

—The Dream of Nebuchadnezzar (Daniel 2:31-35,44, RSV)

The contents of this chapter will come to you as no great surprise if you have read without exception all of the pages in this work. The reason for this is that the motif of this closing chapter has been adumbrated in the preceding pages like clues dropped along the evolutionary pathway of a mystery novel as it approaches its crescendo: Bits and pieces of the conclusion to this chapter have been strewn and sprinkled as literary spice upon the morsels of contemplation served in the temperate syntax before us. Indeed, the final disentangling intricacies of the plot called "the mystery of God" have been deposited in the penumbras of the prominent issues suggested by the titles of the preceding chapters. Unlike the vague or tertiary effect that accompanies any cameo, it is now time to divulge *in toto* the prima facie evidence of the hermeneutical principal employed and assumed in this work which drives the hypothesis contained herein. It is time to look once again at the image of the successive kingdoms in the dream of King Nebuchadnezzar.

In chapter two it was demonstrated that King Nebuchadnezzar's dream of the final and eternal "kingdom of gold," which would eventually replace the last, man-made kingdom on earth (the ten-nation federacy), was the eschatological kingdom of God which is to be established at the end of human history as we know it. It was said that King Nebuchadnezzar's dream adumbrated the eschatological kingdom of God now in the process of embryonic development, to become actually and literally the governing authority of all that takes place "under the whole heaven" (Daniel 7:27). So, regarding this, the following points of clarification are now in order:

1. The final and eternal kingdom of God adumbrated in King Nebuchadnezzar's dream is to be taken as synonymous with the neologisms promulgated in this work as "the ruling, reigning body of Christ," and "the Manchild." "The Manchild" is therefore to be taken as a synonym for the phrase "eternal kingdom of God," which is also to be taken as synonymous with the phrase "the ruling, reigning body of Christ." King Nebuchadnezzar's dream, then, was promoted hereinbefore as an adumbration of the ruling, reigning body of Christ, alias the Manchild.

2. The "kingdom of gold," as the final and eternal "kingdom of God," was metaphorically portrayed as the head of the image in King Nebuchadnezzar's dream. The head of the image was made of gold. In chapter five, Jesus was equated with the head of the image made of gold in King Nebuchadnezzar's dream. Indeed, it was said, Jesus has been commonly referred to as the head of the body, the Church. The image of the head of gold therefore adumbrates Christ as head of the body of true believers.

3. While the dream of King Nebuchadnezzar was decreed to be a vision given by God of the final, eternal, and everlasting kingdom of God, the vision of the birth of the Manchild by John the Revelator was also adjudicated to be a vision given by God of the same kingdom. The conclusion, then, to the evidence put forth in chapters one and two was that this was no mere coincidence, that we should not simply jettison this similarity as happenstance. Instead it was suggested that we should explore the possibility that God is attempting to tell us something that is so incredible and iconoclastic that it would cause in us the response to sit erect and pay full attention. Indeed, such an exploration reveals, as it was posited hereinbefore, that the adumbration in the Book of Daniel serves more than just a foreshadowing of the final and everlasting kingdom of God: It adumbrates what has been popularly called the rapture of the saints of God. This chapter will then present closing arguments on this hypothesis.

4. While it may appear that the Scriptures are mixing metaphors, King Nebuchadnezzar's dream of the final and eternal kingdom of gold serves two purposes: One, the gold head of the body of the image in King Nebuchadnezzar's dream adumbrates Christ as the head of the body; and two, while the final kingdom represented by the head of gold adumbrates Christ as the head of the body, it simultaneously adumbrates the entire ruling, reigning body of Christ which is to rule with Him over all that is under the heavens. It must be remembered, however, that an adumbration does not necessarily serve to specifically clarify or particularize: adumbrations merely point vaguely in a general direction of understanding, which in this case, when interpreted in light of other Scriptures, thereby assumes the authority of an hermeneutical tool. Which therefore leads us to the fifth and final consideration.

5. While the image of the successive kingdoms in the dream of King Nebuchadnezzar adumbrates the eventual establishment of the ruling, reigning body of Christ; and while the image of the successive kingdoms in the dream of King Nebuchadnezzar also mixes literary metaphors in regards specifically to the final kingdom of the gold head, it nevertheless still represents an adumbration of the ruling, reigning body of Christ in the true sense of the word. Thus, being an image which vaguely defines a significant eschatological event, it becomes necessary to exploit it in order to derive from it meaning,

significance, and relevant implications. This exploitation is the intent of this chapter.

In chapter five it was said that John the Revelator, under the inspiration of the Holy Spirit, extended the metaphorical representation of the eternal, everlasting kingdom of God adumbrated by King Nebuchadnezzar's vision, by equating its advent, epiphany, and establishment with the process of human birthing. While the concept of "the body of believers" was acknowledged not to be an unfamiliar concept to readers of the New Testament, what was implicated to be unique about John the Revelator's vision was that it equated the epiphany of the ruling, reigning body with the concept of the birth of a human body. Scripture was then quoted which showed the fleshly metaphorical image of the everlasting kingdom of God in King Nebuchadnezzar's dream:

You saw, O king, and behold, a great image. This image, mighty and of exceeding brightness, stood before you, and its appearance was frightening. The head of this image was of fine gold, its breast and arms of silver, its belly and thighs of bronze, its legs of iron, its feet partly of iron and partly of clay (Daniel 2:31-33, RSV).

While the metaphorical representation of the ruling, reigning body is indubitably tied to John the Revelator's vision of the birth of the Manchild consisting of a head, breast and arms, belly and thighs, legs and feet, it may be beneficial to take a short diversionary excursion here to take notice of the usage of the symbolic metals—gold, silver, bronze, and iron and clay—which are intimately tied to each of these body parts.

In this pericope out of the Book of Daniel, the usage of metals is recognized in the field of hermeneutics as an emblematic prophetic device. However, the usage of metals can rarely be determined to carry symbolism suggestive of another meaning, like the usage of the symbols in Revelation 12:1ff ("the Manchild" as the ruling, reigning body in eternity; "the woman" as the nation of Israel; and "the dragon" as representing Satan). Of all the emblematic elements used in prophetic biblical literature, metals are the most difficult to interpret. They are usually found in lists. In Daniel 2:31-45, for example, the vision of King Nebuchadnezzar apparently displays a purposeful hierarchy of monetary value, from highest to lowest (gold, silver, bronze, iron, and mixture of iron and clay), reflective, of the inherent worth of the kingdom of God (gold). Inherent worth, in this case, seems to be a clue which points to a symbolic meaning: the final and eternal kingdom of God is to be valued highest. We cannot be certain, however, of the meaning and significance of the employment of this list of metals in the dream of King Nebuchadnezzar beyond this simple valuation. Nevertheless, the implications of their usage can be extrapolated: wherein lies the hermeneutical principal employed and assumed in this work which drives the hypothesis contained in the same.

The image of the successive kingdoms in the dream of King Nebuchadnezzar consists of five parts, each associated with a certain symbolic metal. There is the head of gold. There is the breast of the body made of silver. There is the belly of bronze. There are the two legs of iron. And there are the two feet made of iron and clay. Five body parts. Five symbolic metals. Five kingdoms. This image, representing the successive kingdoms which would transpire until the time of the establishment of the ruling, reigning body of Christ, was so impressive to King Nebuchadnezzar that he idolized it by building a replica of it on the plain of Dura, in Babylon:

King Nebuchadnezzar made an image of gold, whose height was sixty cubits and its breadth six cubits. He set it up on the plain of Dura, in the province of Babylon. Then King Nebuchadnezzar sent to assemble the satraps, the prefects, and the governors, the counselors, the treasurers, the justices, the magistrates, and all the officials of the provinces to come to the dedication of the image which King Nebuchadnezzar had set up. Then the satraps, the prefects, and the governors, the counselors, the treasurers, the justices, the magistrates, and all the officials of the provinces, were assembled for the dedication of the image that King Nebuchadnezzar had set up; and they stood before the image that Nebuchadnezzar had set up. And the herald proclaimed aloud, "You are commanded, O peoples, nations, and languages, that when you hear the sound of the horn, pipe, lyre, trigon, harp, bagpipe, and every kind of music, you are to fall down and worship the golden image that King Nebuchadnezzar has set up; and whoever does not fall down and worship shall immediately be cast into a burning fiery furnace." Therefore, as soon as all the peoples heard the sound of the horn, pipe, lyre, trigon, harp, bagpipe, and every kind of music, all the peoples, nations, and languages fell down and worshiped the golden image which King Nebuchadnezzar had set up (Daniel 3:1-7, RSV).

It was toward this image which the Prophet Daniel, and his celebrated coterie of Hebrew friends, would not bow down and worship. Daniel, having pleased King Nebuchadnezzar by the remembrance and interpretation of the dream—which, one, the king could not remember upon his wakening; and two, no other could remember and interpret; and three, which provided the substance for the construction of the replica in the first place—would become *persona non grata*, being cast along with his motley crew of devoted followers of Yahweh into the blazing inferno of the fiery furnace. A number of relevant implications can now be extracted.

Implication Number One

In the dream of the image representing the successive kingdoms, there are five body parts, five symbolic metals, and five kingdoms. This work has also shown that there also are five rapture events. The first rapture was the ascension of Christ. This first rapture is adumbrated by the image of King Nebuchadnezzar's dream: The head of gold of the body of the image is Christ Himself, a separate kingdom, a separate rapture event. The second, third and fourth raptures represent, respectively, the birth of the breast of the body of sliver, the so-called pretribulation saints; the birth of the belly made of bronze, the first group of tribulation saints; and the birth of the legs of iron, the second group of tribulation saints: three separate kingdoms in the dream of King Nebuchadnezzar, three separate parts of the body of the image, but three separate rapture events in reality. The fifth and final rapture then represents the birth of the two feet of the image in the dream of King Nebuchadnezzar, the rapture of the two witnesses. In any normal birthing process, the feet are given birth last. So Scripture decreed that the ministry of the two witnesses would be the last ever over the face of the earth. When the two witnesses are raptured, when the two feet have been given birth, the entire Manchild will have been born; the entire baby is born.

The image in the dream of King Nebuchadnezzar adumbrates the birth of the Manchild as the ruling, reigning body of Christ. But, as has been established *ante*, "the birth" is the rubric under which the concept of the rapture of the saints of God is subsumed. The adumbration of the birth of the Manchild *ipso facto* is the adumbration of the five rapture sequences. This adumbration therefore represents the quintessence of the mystery of God, which is God's plan to repopulate that vacancy created in the ageless past when a third of the heavenly host of angels was excommunicated from the heavenly realm with the Archangel Lucifer when he attempted to become like God. The Manchild at its birth shall represent that company of believers which shall comprise the ruling, reigning body of the eternal kingdom of heaven at the end of time. The Manchild will represent the *magnum opus* of the mystery of God. At its birth, the Manchild shall represent the climax, culmination, consummation, and conclusion of the mystery of God. The adumbration of the birth of the Manchild is therefore the substance of the mystery because the concept of the adumbration predicts the birth of the Manchild contained within the mystery of God, such that the birth of the Manchild decrees that the mystery of God has been realized *in toto*. When the Manchild has been given birth, its birth will signal the completed work of God, heretofore hidden within the concept of the mystery of God. The birth of the Manchild adjudicates that the final chapter of earthly human history has been written. The birth of the Manchild is therefore the denouement of the mystery of God, the final disentangling of the intricacies of the plot called the mystery of God by the Holy Scriptures themselves.

Implication Number Two

The metaphorical representation of the establishment of the eternal kingdom of God as the birth of a body called the Manchild stresses a neglected nuance of the meaning of certain words captured by the colloquial usage of such phrases as "born again" and, by extension, being "saved." These colloquialisms of Christianity have failed at the point of being misused if not ill-defined, such that being "born again" is often taken as a cognate to being "saved." While each of these terms possesses a separate and distinctive nuance, it is not now pertinent to the project at hand to enter into such discourse. What is pertinent, however, is the stressing of the common high ground representative of both terms. This commonality can be reckoned by the compendious three-fold economy of a definition which beholds significant nuances in the past, present, and future tenses of its employment.

Past Tense When Christ died on the cross nearly two thousand years ago, His death established the means for men and women to become "saved," and to become "born again." This is an indisputable fact. However, in order to stress the implications of the past tense, it could be said (though it certainly is not possible) that were no man or woman ever to receive Christ as lord and savior, His death would be for naught. This hypothetical case simply points out that salvation and rebirth are radical in that their roots are intimately and necessarily traced to Calvary at Golgotha. The definition of the phrase referring to being "saved" and being "born again" possesses the past tense nuance of an action performed by Christ Himself. It is only when the historical past tense of the action of Christ is exploited existentially by men and women that salvation and rebirth become personal and therefore existential; i.e., present tense.

Present Tense At that moment when Christ is first embraced as Lord and Savior through the work of the Holy Spirit through prevenient grace, the traditional and popular understanding of the words being "saved" and being "born again" applies. Whereas the past tense reckons an action by Christ, the present tense considers the act of the will of men and women to elect to surrender themselves to the lordship and messiahship of Christ. But being "saved" implies being rescued from something, namely, the wrath of God. While it is coherent to talk about being freed from the necessity of sin each day, the purpose of such cessation is nevertheless future-directed. Being "born again" implies that at some futuristic point in time, we shall be raptured and placed in the eternal security of the ruling, reigning body of Christ.

While we are not literally saved from anything yet except that we have suspended sinning in order to possess an existential security of gaining membership in the eternal kingdom of God, and while we are not literally raptured yet, the intrinsic intent in any conversion experience is that we shall remain eternally in Christ by the power of the

Holy Spirit until such time as we are placed into the eternal security of perpetual salvation as members in perpetuity of the kingdom of God which is yet to come. Just as the past tense meaning of the usage of the terms "born again" and "saved" refer to an action completed by Christ; and as the present tense of the meaning of the same words implies an act of volition on the part of men and women to remain in Christ by the power of the Holy Spirit, we are therefore confronted with the possibility that a man having elected to follow Christ through his conversion experience may elect to reverse that decision by stepping out of the protection of Christ. He does so by being *lured and enticed by his own desire* for sin (James 1: 14, RSV). To say that I am now a married man does not mean that I will always be a married man. It means, barring extenuating circumstances, that so long as I work at keeping the marriage healthy I shall remain a married man. To say that I am a happily married man assumes that I will continue to work at this marriage, and that I hope to remain in such a state of harmony in the future. The teleology of conversion is to repopulate that vacancy created in the ageless past when a third of the heavenly host of angels was excommunicated from the heavenly realm. Naturally, then, the hope of conversion in the present tense is that we should remain in Christ through the power of the Holy Spirit; that we should endure to the end. Indeed, as we have already quoted, "he who endures to the end shall be saved." It would therefore be foolish for us to consider, when employing the terms "saved" and "born again," that we did not possess a futuristic hope of what the terms imply.

So when I say that I am "saved," I do not mean that I am already saved from the wrath of God because the wrath of God has not yet come: it means that I have suspended sinning through the power of the Holy Spirit in order that when Christ returns in one of His rapture appearances, I may be found doing the will of God and thus be placed in the eternal security of His loving protection. And when I say that I am "born again," I do not mean that I am already raptured into the eternal security of perpetual salvation as a member in perpetuity of the kingdom of God. What I really mean when I say that I am "saved" and "born again" is that today I am in Christ (if I am not sinning); that so long as I remain in Christ, doing the will of God as He beckons by the power of the Holy Spirit, then I shall be saved from His wrath and eventually gain eternal security as a member in perpetuity of the kingdom of God. Obviously then, a third and future tense of the words "saved" and "born again" is implied.

Future Tense While the past tense signals an act completed by Christ, and the present tense enjoins the exercise of the human will, the future tense adjudicates an act of the Most High God. This third temporal aspect of the usage of the words "saved" and "born again" represents the predestined state of the believer. All of creation history longs for the transformation of this present world order into the futurity of the eternal order of bliss. The impending implications of the nuance of being "saved" and "born again" represent our hopes residing in a destination in eternity. The eschatological realization of the hereafter is our ultimate *raison d'etre*. When the birth of the Manchild is consummated, those who have endured to the end shall immediately and eternally be caught up into the security of perpetual membership in the kingdom of God. This will represent the ultimate "rebirth," the ultimate state of being "born again" as members of the body of the Manchild. Our "salvation" will be from the wrath of God which will be poured out upon those *who do not know God and upon those who do not obey the gospel of our lord Jesus* (1 Thessalonians 1:8, RSV). Once the birth of the Manchild as the ruling, reigning body of Christ has been realized, no more may be added to the body of Christ. Once the Manchild is born, no other will ever possess opportunity to gain entrance into the body of Christ. The birth of the Manchild as the ruling, reigning body of Christ is therefore the denouement of the mystery of God. It is our hope, our rebirth, our salvation. Praise be to God through His Son Jesus for whom we owe our entire lives for granting wretched sinners an opportunity, if we remain in Him, to not only live eternally in His presence, but to partake of the regency of ruling all that is under the heavens in the New Jerusalem, the eternal city of God.

Appendix I

The Second Coming

As Jesus sat on the Mount of Olives, the disciples came to him privately, saying, "Tell us, when will this be, and what will be the sign of your coming and of the close of the age?" "For as the lightning comes from the east and shines as far as the west, so will be the coming of the Son of man. Wherever the body is, there the eagles will be gathered together. Immediately after the tribulation of those days the sun will be darkened, and the moon will not give its light, and the stars will fall from heaven, and the powers of the heavens will be shaken; then will appear the sign of the Son of man in heaven, and then all the tribes of the earth will mourn, and they will see the Son of man coming on the clouds of heaven with power and great glory. From the fig tree learn its lesson: as soon as its branch becomes tender and puts forth its leaves, you know that summer is near. So also, when you see all these things, you know that He is near, at the very gates.

—Jesus of Nazareth (Matthew 24:3,27-30,32-33, RSV)

For some it is interesting to study the historical linguistic changes in certain words which have evolved into popular usage in the English language. This is known as the discipline of etymology. In chapter four, a pithy etymology was given for the word "rapture," which, it was said therein, is a word not found in the Bible but nevertheless is loaded with meaning and significance for the human race. An important English phrase which is not found in the Bible is the phrase "second coming." Like the word "rapture," "second coming" is packed with great mystery and meaning. In order to understand it, it will be necessary to "unpack" its meaning, which is a process sometimes aided by the study of the word's historical linguistic changes. It is regrettable that the usage of "second coming" possesses a cognate deleterious history similar to the academic usage of the word "metaphysics."

"Metaphysics" was the title given by Aristotle's editors to a sub-section of one of his literary works. This sub-section, entitled *Metaphysics*, was labeled by Aristotle as his *First Philosophy*. (This no doubt represents the first recorded battle of the infamous editor-writer war which persists even to this day.) Aristotles *First Philosophy* attempted to determine how the universe first came into existence. Hence the word *First* in *First Philosophy*. This piece of intellectually stimulating material was presented in the final section of Aristotle's book. It was a serious but entirely distinct break from the traditional treatment of physics in the earlier section of his book. (The first part of Aristotle's book consisted of his elaborations on the so-called hard sciences of physics. The last section dealt with a subject matter more appropriately subsumed under the rubric, "soft sciences;" i.e., philosophical investigation. Philosophers of antiquity saw no great separation between the hard and soft sciences, as do the modern peddlers of hard-core, radical empiricism who belittle the role of the King Philosophers of antiquity.) Aristotle's editors were Greek, and the Greek word *meta* means after. So out of expediency the editors called this section *Metaphysics* merely to refer to the physical location of Aristotle's *First Philosophy*. The editors were therefore simply referring to those final pages as "that which comes after the discussion of physics." Meta physics. After physics.

Well the word stuck, but from that day forward, the precise scope of metaphysical inquiry became difficult to define, its exact meaning remaining uncertain to this day (which is why the definition of the word was supplied in a footnote when it was first used in chapter two). Without clearly defining the range of meanings of certain words which linger nondescript in the minds of those who desire to understand them, the reader is left in a quandary of sorts, unable to grasp the authorial intent of the word's usage, which necessarily results in a loss of effective communication. When either the precise scope of a word's meaning becomes difficult to define or is not defined at all, or the peculiar nuances of such go undetected, its usage thereby remains not only nearly useless as it lies couched in a manner of uncertainty, but when it is used, it tends to generate a whirlwind of confusion whose origin can be traced to its misunderstanding. The meaning of the words "rapture" and "second coming" are in a like manner misunderstood in the minds of Christians. While certain aspects of their meanings have been correctly apprehended, it is the peculiar nuances of each which go undetected that become the source of the whirlwinds of confusion which are normally associated with the controversies contained thereabout. In the cases of the uses of the words "rapture" and "second coming," the whirlwinds of confusion are in part generated by the rigid and restrictive theological bias characteristic of the camp out of which the user or reader emerges: pre-millennialist, mid-millennialist, post-millennialist, a-millennialist, pretribulation, mid-tribulation, post-tribulation, *ad infinitum, ad nauseam*. It is therefore in our best interest to establish the range of acceptable meanings to the likes of such words as "rapture," and "second coming." So, having already considered the meaning of the word "rapture" in chapter four, it is now time to consider the meaning of "second coming."

The Traditional Understanding of the Second Coming

The essence of consensual agreement by the varying theological schools of thought, representing the traditional understanding of the event we are calling the second coming of Christ, is that it is an eschatological event wherein Jesus will physically return to the earth at a time understood to be sometime after His ascension. The quintessence of the second coming is therefore restricted to be the return of Christ to earth to accomplish whatever it is that He intends to do at the time of His return. After that it is, as they say, up for grabs. The timing of His second coming depends upon whether one's interpretive paradigm is represented by the nomenclature of the pre-, mid-, post-, or a-millennial model. What events unfold during the second coming depends upon the theological bias of the theologian considering its implications, which is itself intimately tied to the various millennial interpretations suggested above. This conundrum should be expected, however, about a theological issue which is supported by a paucity of Scripture. But perplexity is not a necessity of paucity. Even though there simply is not a great deal of scriptural reference about the second coming, it is still possible to weave a thread of understanding which ties together what appears to be a variety of scriptural anomalies. (It must be remembered that another critical doctrine of scripture is reflected by a "paucity of scriptural justification:" the doctrine of the trinity.) Since there is some agreement about what will take place during the second rapture, it would therefore be worthy to begin with this common ground. And then it would serve us well to examine the usage of the Greek word which gives us the concept of the second coming. But first, a look at the traditional understanding of the concept of the second coming is in order. This, too, is represented by a limited but sufficient common theological ground.

A Limited Common Ground

From the various but scant scriptural references which deal almost obliquely with the substance of His second coming, only the following collage of events can be ascertained (no chronological sequence herein suggested): a time of punishment upon Jerusalem; a time of punishment upon the wicked (in the mother of all battles); a time of judgment upon the living and the dead; a time of terminating this world's order as preparation for the next; and a time of transporting redeemed humanity into the resurrection life of heaven, better known as the rapture, or what has been called in this work the birth of the Manchild as the ruling, reigning body of Christ.

The Greek Word Parousia

Since the scope of scriptural references to the second coming is limited, it will then be necessary to turn to additional hermeneutical devices which may help shed light upon this important spiritual event. One such device is the examination of the original language out of which the concept arises. The Greek word typically associated with the second coming, which is simply translated "coming" in our English Bible, is the word *parousia*. Some Greek words have become incorporated into the English language without the benefit of English translation; i.e., they have simply become transliterated. *Parousia* is one of these words. Even though its English definition is "coming," it has become fashionable to use the Greek word itself in place of its definition. It is a common Christian term which is often used synonymously with the phrase "the second coming" or "the Second Advent." The transliterated word *parousia*, however, having made it into our English vocabulary, has not come to be used without some risk: it has lost some of its meaning. We cannot blame this loss entirely upon a simple transliteration: the dilution of meaning also must be credited to a neglect of the important and distinctive nuances possessed by the concept it determines. A cursory deductive investigation of the Greek word *parousia* is therefore in order.

The word *parousia* occurs just twenty-tmo times in the entire Greek New Testament. Its occurrence can be cataloged in the following capacity:[1]

* In four of these twenty-two occurrences, the word *parousia* refers to the coming of mere mortals in the personages of Stephanas, Fortunatus, Achaicus, Titus, and the apostle Paul (1 Cor 16:17; 2 Cor 7:6,7; Phil 1:26). Judging from these four occurrences alone, it is necessary to concede that the use of the Greek word *parousia* is not restricted to a description of the event which is popularly called the second coming.

* Of the remaining sixteen occurrences of the word *parousia*, eight clearly refer to the event which we have just labeled in chapter six as the second rapture (1 Corinthians 15:23; 1 Thessalonians 2:19, 4:15, 5:23, 2 Thessalonians 2:1; James 5:7-8; 1 John 2:28).

* It is out of the remaining nine occurrences of the word *parousia*, then, that eight of them indisputably refer to the event which is

---

1. See Appendix III for the inclusive listing of each of these occurrences. Of the twenty-two occurrences of the word *parousia*, eight verses occur in six Pauline texts, four verses in one Matthew pericope, three verses in 2 Peter, two verses in one Jamesian text, and one verse in 1 John. The remaining four occur in reference to the visits of mere mortals.

otherwise known as the second coming (Matthew 24:3-39; 1 Thessalonians 3:13; and 2 Thessalonians 2:8-9; 2 Peter 3:12).

* The final two of these twenty-two occurrences (2 Peter 1:6, 3:4) could refer to either the second rapture or the second coming. The subject matter in each of them concerns itself with living the Christian life, which means that the *parousia*—whether the second rapture or the second coming—is only marginally implicated.

From this cursory deductive investigation of the Greek word *parousia*, it can be concluded that the word *parousia* refers to three distinct types of coming:

* the arrival of mere mortal men (which carries with it no eschatological function);

* the arrival of Christ at the second rapture of the saints;

* the arrival of Christ as a sort of grand finale, toting His ruling, reigning body at His side.

There are other passages of Scripture which refer to a coming of Christ to earth, which employ Greek new testament words other than *parousia*. Some of them are: *erchomai* (e. g., Mark 13:36; Acts 1:11; Matthew 25:31; 1 Thessalonians 5:2; Revelation 16:15); *apokalupsis* (e.g., 2 Thessalonians 1:7); *heko* (e.g., 2 Peter 3:10); and *katabaino* (e.g., 1 Thessalonians 4:16).

And from a cursory deductive investigation of these examples, it can be concluded that they also refer to three distinct types of coming:

* the arrival of mere mortal men (which carries with it no eschatological function);

* the arrival of Christ at the second rapture of the saints;

* the arrival of Christ as a sort of Grand Finale, toting His ruling, reigning body at His side.

Of course there are other words in other texts which refer to the coming of Christ, but this simple deductive examination possesses sufficient evidence to demand the following conclusion: The second coming is not synonymous with the second rapture.

The Greek word *parousia* has been shown to refer to the arrival of mere mortals. It also has been shown to possess a significant nuance which refers to the second coming of Christ (with whatever that entails). Then there is that third significant nuance of the definition of the word *parousia*: an appearance of Jesus which is not related to His historically defined second coming. This is the nuance of neglect. This is the nuance of nonrecognition. This is the nuance of reticence. But it is the nuance which can be exploited for the sake of scriptural clarity. It is the nuance with an implication which becomes, as we will see, the key for resolving the trichotomous theological confusion surrounding the role of the rapture in the pre-trib, mid-trib and post-trib models. And it is the nuance which can be sacrificed upon the altar of understanding to demonstrate the means of the birth of the Manchild as the ruling, reigning body of Christ in eternity.

In the confusion surrounding most issues, there always are elements of truth contained therein. These are the nuances which are correctly apprehended which lend credence to the issues at hand. In the case of the use of the Greek word *parousia*, one nuance of the meaning of the word is the traditional certainty of a final General Judgment which will mark the end of the present world order and the entry of redeemed humanity into the resurrection life of heaven. The specifics of that denouement, however; indeed, the disentangling of the final pieces to the mystery of God, have eluded the Church up to this point. The clarification of this confusion could be contained within the "paradigm of multiple raptures," suggested in part by one of the following: deductive investigation of the word *parousia*, by John the Revelator's vision of the birth of the Manchild; by the adumbration of the image of the beast in King Nebuchadnezzar's dream. Before we are able to take another look at King Nebuchadnezzar's dream, it will be necessary to exploit first the neglected nuances of the concepts determined by the use of the words *parousia* and rapture. This will, however, require a maturation of the old paradigm we have been using in the past to interpret Scripture: The need to make a theological distinction between *a parousia* of Christ and *the parousia* of Christ (discounting, of course, the *parousia* of mere mortals mentioned earlier). It also will require making a theological distinction between a single rapture event and the possibility of more than one rapture events to secure a population of saints into the ruling, reigning body of Christ.

A Paradigm Shift: Another Look at the Word Rapture

The Greek word for "rapture," as previously given in chapter four, is *harpazo* (har-pad'-zo), meaning simply "to seize." It is used just twelve times throughout the entire Greek New Testament.[2] Like the word *parousia*, not every use of it is tied to that event which has come to be called "the rapture." Indeed, in only two of the dozen times *harpazo* is used, does it refer to the so-called rapture of the saints (1 Thessalonians 4:17; Revelation 12:5). As in the cases of the paucity of Scripture justifying the doctrines of the trinity and the second coming, the two sole uses of the Greek word *harpazo* do not therefore prohibit the integrity of the doctrine spun out of them. The issue is not in the conditional premise, "if the rapture is justifiable;" it is in the dependent and resultant conclusion which begs the following question: "What, then, are the theological implications of the rapture?"

In this work, the concept of the birth of the Manchild has been promulgated as the divine means of creating a population of saints to inhabit the eternal kingdom of God. The birth of the Manchild has been equated with the establishment of the ruling, reigning body of Christ which will rule with Him over the kingdom which is to come. So the birth of the Manchild is the metaphorical means of "adding to the body of Christ" (Acts 2:47; 5:14; 11:24; 1 Corinthians 12:27). "The birth," as it was established in chapter four, is to be taken as a synonym for "the rapture." Indeed, in Revelation 12:5, the rapture alias the birth of the entire body is represented by the use of the Greek word *harpazo*: *And the woman brought forth a Manchild, who was to rule all nations with a rod of iron: and her child was caught up (harpazo) unto God, and to His throne.*

---

2. See Appendix IV for a complete listing of these verses.

So the rapture is the divine means for taking true believers—whether dead or alive—and putting them in the eternal security of the body of Christ. Jesus the head of the body was raptured at His ascension. Those that have died in the Lord thereinafter will be raptured—though dead—during the second rapture. And those true believers who are yet alive at His second rapture coming will also be "seized," "caught up," or "raptured" into the body of Christ.

But what about those post-second rapture saints who come to sincere faith in Christ during the period of the tribulation? How will they be added to the body of Christ?

What is unique about the employment of the only two uses of the Greek word *harpazo*, which refer to the traditional concept known as the rapture, Christ is present at this spiritually significant event. As a matter of fact, in one of these two verses, namely, Revelation 12:5, the entire population of saints which will comprise the ruling, reigning body is "added to the Lord" through the process of the birth von the rapture von *harpazo*. And since Christ is present at the rapture of the entire population of saints which will constitute the Manchild, it therefore follows that He also must be present in some capacity when the post-second rapture saints are added to the entire population of saints which will comprise the ruling, reigning body. Which brings us to the second required maturation of the old paradigm we have used to interpret Scripture in the past.

A Paradigm Shift: Another Look at the Word Parousia

Here, two considerations must be made. One, in each of the occurrences of what we are calling the multiple raptures of the saints, Christ will be visible to the saints He is plucking from the earth. Jesus (obviously) was present during the first rapture, which was His ascension, and the Lord will be visible to the pretribulation saints in the second rapture. But He also will be visible to the mid-tribulation saints who will be raptured during this period. (It should be noted, however, that as the Apostle Paul so described it, each rapture will occur *in a moment, in the twinkling of an eye* (1 Corinthians 15:52, RSV). His appearance or "coming" will be so instantaneous that not only will those who remain on earth not see Him, but it will occur so quickly that he who is raptured will find himself immediately in the presence of God. It may be that in this case of the rapture of the tribulation saints that we are needlessly tripping over a semantic issue: His "coming" during the tribulation raptures, being so instantaneous as they will be, can be taken to be synonymous with finding oneself immediately in the presence of God through the process of being raptured. The appearances of Christ at each of these raptures will therefore represent *a parousia*. But none of them will be *the parousia*.

This brings us to consideration number two: *The parousia*, as we have already concluded *supra*, is not to be taken as synonymous with any part of the birth. This necessarily means it is not to be taken as synonymous with any part of the multiple raptures which will occur to bring an entire population of saints to become the ruling, reigning body of Christ. *The parousia* is to be taken only as synonymous with the second coming, which will be an event which all people, both heathen and Christian, will witness. Christ will be visible only to those saints which He is bringing in for placement in the ruling, reigning body, through a process we are calling the birth alias the rapture. He will not, at each of His rapture appearances, be visible to all the world as is required by the following scriptural mandate of His second coming which comes at a later time:

> *then will appear the sign of the Son of man in heaven, and then all the tribes of the earth will mourn, and they will see the son of man coming on the clouds of heaven with power and great glory. Before him will be gathered all the nations, and he will separate them one from another as a shepherd separates the sheep from the goats* (Matthew 24:30; 25:32, RSV).

So Jesus will be present at each of the various raptures, as one of the nuances of the definition of the Greek word *parousia* indicates, but His presence at each of these raptures will not qualify as *the parousia* of Matthew 25:31-32, alias the second coming of Christ, the second advent, and the Judgment of the world. But once the full number of those whose names are written in the Book of Life are firmly placed in the eternal security of the ruling, reigning body of Christ (through the means of multiple raptures), then *the parousia* will take place: The return of Christ will be at this time with His full body. Together the head and the body of the Manchild shall then descend in full visibility of all eyes, to mete out justice, vengeance, wrath, and judgment.

Appendix II

A Study of the Word *Mystery*

The New Testament Occurrence of the Word Mystery

In the Revised Standard Version (RSV) of the New Testament, the English word "mystery" (and its plural) occurs twenty-three times. In the King James Version (KJV) of the New Testament, the English word "mystery" (and its plural) occurs twenty-seven times. To some, this may provide a discrepancy which diminishes the reliability of the English translations we now have in abundance. However, to those who make their living in the field of biblical languages, this presents no *faux pas,* because the New Testament was written not in English, but in what is known as Koine Greek, the common man's language in the day of Christ. So to pursue word comparisons in the English language would be a lesson in futility, since the original New Testament was written in Greek. We need only look then at the original Greek word underlying the English word "mystery" to secure interpretive integrity in the English translations.

The Greek Word Musterion

The Greek word for "mystery" is *musterion* [moos-tay'-ree-on]. (*Musterion* comes from a derivative of another Greek word, *muo,* which itself means *to shut the mouth.*) The English rendering of the Greek word *musterion* (unanimously accepted by scholars in the field of biblical languages) is "a secret" or "a mystery". The Greek word *musterion* occurs exactly twenty-seven times throughout the entire

Bible, which just so happens to coincide identically with the number of times it occurs as "mystery" in the KJV of the New Testament. So the KJV has simply chosen to translate all twenty-seven occurrences of the Greek word *musterion* as "mystery."

The RSV, on the other hand, has elected to translate the twenty-seven occurrences of the Greek word *musterion* as "mystery" in twenty-three places, and as *secret* in the other four places, since *secret* is an equally acceptable English word equivalent. The RSV, then, has simply chosen the English equivalent "secret" instead of "mystery" in four places, but in the Greek text, the word is always *musterion*. It is interesting that the Greek word *musterion* occurs only twenty-seven times in the entire Greek New Testament, the preponderant usage indubitably adumbrating the mystery of God, the hidden, eternal plan of God that is being revealed to God's people in accordance with His plan.

Old Testament Occurrence of Mystery

In the King James Version of the Old Testament, the English word "mystery" does not occur even once. In the Revised Standard Version of the Old Testament, the English word "mystery" occurs eight times. Again, to some, this may provide a discrepancy which diminishes the reliability of the English translations we have at our disposal but, as in the case of the New Testament, to those who make their living in the field of biblical languages, this also represents no *faux pas*, because the Old Testament was not written in English either, but primarily in Hebrew, with a few sections written in Aramaic. As a matter of fact, the text from which the Prophet Daniel recounts King Nebuchadnezzar's dream is written totally in Aramaic. So to pursue word comparisons in the English language would also be a lesson in futility, since the text which we are examining was originally written in Aramaic. We need only look, then, at the original Aramaic word underlying the English word "mystery" in the RSV Old Testament to secure interpretive integrity in the English translation.

The Aramaic Word Raz

The Aramaic word underlying the RSV word for "mystery" is *raz* [rawz]. Apparently it comes from an unused word root which probably means to attenuate, that is, to figuratively hide. The English definition of the Aramaic word *raz* unanimously accepted by scholars in the field of biblical languages is "mystery." The Aramaic word *raz* occurs exactly eight times throughout the entire Bible, coinciding with the eight occurrences where the RSV renders it "mystery". The KJV Old Testament, on the other hand, carries no single occurrences of the English word "mystery." While it is true that the English word "mystery" does not occur even once in the KJV Old Testament, the English word "secret" does; it occurs exactly eight times, in the identical locations where the RSV renders *raz* "mystery." Evidently the interpreters of the KJV elected to employ a cognate definition of the English word "mystery," namely "secret." That is to say that the KJV version has simply translated the Aramaic word raz as "secret," and the RSV has simply translated the same Aramaic word *raz* as "mystery."

What is interesting to note here is not only that there are no more than eight occurrences of the words "secret" (KJV) and "mystery" (RSV) in the entire Old Testament, but that all of the occurrences of this word are contained within the Book of Daniel. Furthermore, of the eight occurrences of this word throughout the entire Bible, which happen to occur only in the Book of Daniel, all of them are in reference to King Nebuchadnezzar's dream, which we have been calling the adumbration of the mystery of the Manchild, the hidden, eternal plan of God that is now being revealed to us in accordance with His plan.

In what now follows will be a simple display of parallel occurrences of the words "mystery" and "secret" as they occur in the King James Version and the Revised Standard Version.

Four occurrences of Greek *musterion*
where KJV elects "mystery" and RSV elects "secret"
English equivalents are in Roman type.

Matthew 13:11

KJV *He answered and said unto them, Because it is given unto you to know the* mysteries *of the kingdom of heaven, but to them it is not given.*

RSV *And He answered them, "To you it has been given to know the* secrets *of the kingdom of heaven, but to them it has not been given."*

Mark 4:11

KJV *And he said unto them, Unto you it is given to know the* mystery *of the kingdom of God: but unto them that are without, all these things are done in parables:*

RSV *And He said to them, "To you it has been given the* secret *of the kingdom of God, but for those outside everything is in parables;"*

Luke 8:10

KJV *And he said, Unto you it is given to know the* mysteries *of the kingdom of God: but to others in parables; that seeing they might not see, and hearing they might not understand.*

RSV *He said, "To you it has been given to know the* secrets *of the kingdom of God; but for others they are in parables,"*

1 Corinthians 2:7

KJV *But we speak the wisdom of God in a* mystery, *even the hidden wisdom, which God ordained before the world unto our glory:*

RSV *But we impart a* secret *and hidden wisdom of God, which God decreed before the ages for our glorification.*

Twenty-three occurrences of Greek *musterion*
where both KJV and RSV elect "mystery"

Romans 11:25

KJV *For I would not, brethren, that ye should be ignorant of this* mystery, *lest ye should be wise in your own conceits; that blindness in part is happened to Israel, until the fullness of the Gentiles be come in.*

RSV *Lest you be wise in your own conceits, I want you to understand this* mystery, *brethren: a hardening has come upon part of Israel, until the full number of the Gentiles come in.*

Romans 16:25

KJV *Now to him that is of power to stablish you according to my gospel, and the preaching of Jesus Christ, according to the revelation of the* mystery, *which was kept secret since the world began.*

RSV *Now to him who is able to strengthen you according to my gospel and the preaching of Jesus Christ, according to the revelation of the* mystery *which was kept secret for long ages.*

1 Cor 4:1

KJV *Let a man so account of us, as of the ministers of Christ, and stewards of the* mysteries *of God.*

RSV *This is how one should regard us, as servants of Christ and stewards of the* mysteries *of God.*

1 Cor 13:2

KJV *And though I have the gift of prophecy, and understand all* mysteries, *and all knowledge; and though I have all faith, so that I could remove mountains, and have not charity, I am nothing.*

RSV *And if I have prophetic powers, and understand all* mysteries *and all knowledge, and if I have all faith, so as to remove mountains, but have not love, I am nothing.*

1 Cor 14:2

KJV *For he that speaketh in an unknown tongue speaketh not unto men, but unto God: for no man understandeth him; howbeit in the spirit he speaketh* mysteries.

RSV *For one who speaks in a tongue speaks not to men but to God; for no one understands him, but he utters* mysteries *in the Spirit.*

1 Cor 15:51

KJV *Behold, I shew you a* mystery; *We shall not all sleep, but we shall all be changed.*

RSV *Lo! I tell you a* mystery. *We shall not all sleep, but we shall all be changed.*

Eph 1:9

KJV *Having made known unto us the* mystery *of his will, acccording to his good pleasure which he hath purposed in himself:*

RSV *For he has made known to us in all wisdom and insight the* mystery *of his will, according to his purpose which he set forth in Christ.*

Eph 3:3

KJV *How that by revelation he made known unto me the* mystery; *(as I wrote afore in few words.*

RSV *How the* mystery *was made known to me by revelation, as I have written briefly.*

Eph 3:4

KJV *Whereby, when ye read, ye may understand my knowledge in the* mystery *of Christ).*

RSV *When you read this you can perceive my insight into the* mystery *of Christ.*

Eph 3:9

KJV *And to make all men see what is the fellowship of the* mystery, *which from the beginning of the world hath been hid in God, who created all things by Jesus Christ:*

RSV *and to make all men see what is the plan of the* mystery *hidden for ages in God who created all things;*

Eph 5:32

KJV *This is a great* mystery: *but I speak concerning Christ and the church.*

RSV *This* mystery *is a profound one, and I am saying that it refers to Christ and the church;*

Eph 6:19

KJV *And for me, that utterance may be given unto me, that I may open my mouth boldly, to make known the* mystery *of the gospel*

RSV *and also for me, that utterance may be given me in opening my mouth boldly to proclaim the* mystery *of the gospel,*

Col 1:26

KJV *Even the* mystery *which hath been hid from ages and from generations, but now is made manifest to his saints:*

RSV *the* mystery *hidden for ages and generations but now made manifest to his saints.*

Col 1:27

KJV *To whom God would make known what is the riches of the glory of this* mystery *among the Gentiles; which is Christ in you, the hope of glory:*

RSV *To them God chose to make known how great among the Gentiles are the riches of the glory of this* mystery, *which is Christ in you, the hope of glory.*

Col 2:2

KJV *That their hearts might be comforted, being knit together in love, and unto all riches of the full assurance of understanding, to the acknowledgement of the* mystery *of God, and of the Father, and of Christ;*

RSV *that their hearts may be encouraged as they are knit together in love, to have all the riches of assured understanding and the knowledge of God's* mystery, *of Christ,*

Col 4:3

KJV *Withal praying also for us, that God would open unto us a door of utterance, to speak the* mystery *of Christ, for which I am also in bonds:*

RSV *and pray for us also, that God may open to us a door for the word, to declare the* mystery *of Christ, on account of which I am in prison,*

2 Thes 2:7

KJV *For the* mystery *of iniquity doth already work: only he who now letteth will let, until he be taken out of the way.*

RSV *For the* mystery *of lawlessness is already at work; only he who now restrains it will do so until he is out of the way.*

1 Tim 3:9

KJV *Holding the* mystery *of the faith in a pure conscience.*

RSV *they must hold the* mystery *of the faith with a clear conscience.*

1 Tim 3:16

KJV *And without controversy great is the* mystery *of godliness: God was manifest in the flesh, justified in the Spirit, seen of angels, preached unto the Gentiles, believed on in the world, received up into glory.*

RSV *Great indeed, we confess, is the* mystery *of our religion: He was manifested in the flesh, vindicated in the Spirit, seen by angels, preached among the nations, believed on in the world, taken up in glory.*

Rev 1:20

KJV *The* mystery *of the seven stars which thou sawest in my right hand, and the seven golden candlesticks. The seven stars are the angels of the seven churches: and the seven candlesticks which thou sawest are the seven churches.*

RSV *As for the* mystery *of the seven stars which you saw in my right hand, and the seven golden lampstands, the seven stars are the angels of the seven churches and the seven lampstands are the seven churches.*

Rev 10:7

KJV *But in the days of the voice of the seventh angel, when he shall begin to sound, the* mystery *of God should be finished, as he hath declared to his servants the prophets.*

RSV *but that in the days of the trumpet call to be sounded by the seventh angel, the* mystery *of God, as he announced to his servants the prophets, should be fulfilled.*

Rev 17:5

KJV *And upon her forehead was a name written,* mystery, *BABYLON THE GREAT, THE MOTHER OF HARLOTS AND ABOMINATIONS OF THE EARTH.*

RSV *and on her forehead was written a name of* mystery: *"Babylon the great, mother of harlots and of earth's abominations."*

Rev 17:7

KJV *And the angel said unto me, Wherefore didst thou marvel? I will tell thee the* mystery *of the woman, and of the beast that carrieth her, which hath the seven heads and ten horns.*

RSV *But the angel said to me, Why marvel? I will tell you the* mystery *of the woman, and of the beast with seven heads and ten horns that carries her.*

Occurrences of Aramaic *raz*
where KJV elects "secret" and RSV elects "mystery"

Daniel 2:18

KJV *That they would desire mercies of the God of heaven concerning this* secret; *that Daniel and his fellows should not perish with the rest of the wise men of Babylon.*

RSV *and told them to seek mercy of the God of heaven concerning this* mystery, *so that Daniel and his companions might not perish with the rest of the wise men of Babylon*

Daniel 2:19

KJV *Then was the* secret *revealed unto Daniel in a night vision. Then Daniel blessed the God of heaven.*

RSV *when the* mystery *was revealed to Daniel in a vision of the night. Then Daniel blessed the God of heaven*

Daniel 2:27

KJV *Daniel answered in the presence of the king, and said, The* secret *which the king hath demanded cannot the wise men, the astrologers, the magicians, the soothsayers, shew unto the king;*

RSV *Daniel answered the king, "No wise men, enchanters, magicians, or astrologers can show to the king the* mystery *which the king has asked."*

Daniel 2:28

KJV *But there is a God in heaven that revealeth* secrets, *and maketh known to the king Nebuchadnezzar what shall be in the latter days. Thy dream, and the visions of thy head upon thy bed, are these;*

RSV *but there is a God in heaven who reveals* mysteries, *and he has made known to King Nebuchadnez'zar what will be in the latter days. Your dream and the visions of your head as you lay in bed are these:*

Daniel 2:29

KJV *As for thee, O king, thy thoughts came into thy mind upon thy bed, what should come to pass hereafter: and he that revealeth* secrets *maketh known to thee what shall come to pass.*

RSV *To you, O king, as you lay in bed came thoughts of what would be hereafter, and he who reveals* mysteries *made known to you what is to be.*

Daniel 2:30

KJV *But as for me, this* secret *is not revealed to me for any wisdom that I have more than any living, but for their sakes that shall make known the interpretation to the king, and that thou mightest know the thoughts of thy heart.*

RSV *But as for me, not because of any wisdom that I have more than all the living has this* mystery *been revealed to me, but in order that the interpretation may be made known to the king, and that you may know the thoughts of your mind.*

Daniel 2:47

KJV *The king answered unto Daniel, and said, Of a truth it is, that your God is a God of gods, and a Lord of kings, and a revealer* of secrets, *seeing thou couldest reveal this* secret.

RSV *The king said to Daniel, "Truly, your God is God of gods and Lord of kings, and a revealer* of mysteries, *for you have been able to reveal this* mystery."

Daniel 4:9

KJV *O Belteshazzar, master of the magicians, because I know that the spirit of the holy gods is in thee, and no* secret *troubleth thee, tell me the visions of my dream that I have seen, and the interpretation thereof.*

RSV *O Belteshaz'zar, chief of the magicians, because I know that the spirit of the holy gods is in you and that no* mystery *is difficult for you, here is the dream which I saw; tell me its interpretation.*

Appendix III

A Study of the Word *Parousia*

The Greek New Testament occurrence of the Greek word *"parousia"* as they are translated into the English equivalents (KJV). Verse references bracketed—there are three—refer to the coming of mere mortal men. English equivalents are in roman type.

Matt 24:3 *and as He sat upon the mount of Olives, the disciples came unto Him privately, saying, Tell us, when shall these things be? And what shall be the sign of Thy* coming, *and of the end of the world?*

Matt 24:27 *For as the lightning cometh out of the east, and shineth even unto the west; so shall also the* coming *of the Son of man be.*

Matt 24:37 *But as the days of Noah were, so shall also the* coming *of the Son of man be.*

Matt 24:39 *And knew not until the flood came, and took them all away; so shall also the* coming *of the Son of man be.*

1 Cor 15:23 *But every man in his own order: Christ the firstfruits; afterward they that are Christ's at His* coming.

[1 Cor 16:17] *I am glad of the* coming *of Stephanas and Fortunatus and Achaicus: for that which was lacking on your part they have supplied.*

[2 Cor 7:6,7] (two times) *Nevertheless God, that comforteth those that are cast down, comforted us by the* coming *of Titus. And not by his* coming *only, but by the consolation wherewith he was comforted in you, when he told us your earnest desire, your mourning, your fervent mind toward me; so that I rejoiced the more.*

[Phil 1:26] *That your rejoicing may be more abundant in Jesus Christ for me by* [Paul's] coming *to you again.*

1 Thes 2:19 *For what is our hope, or joy, or crown of rejoicing? Are not even ye in the presence of our Lord Jesus Christ at His* coming?

1 Thes 3:13 *To the end He may stablish your hearts unblameable in holiness before God, even our Father, at the* coming *of our Lord Jesus Christ with all His saints.*

1 Thes 4:15 *For this we say unto you by the word of the Lord, that we which are alive and remain unto the* coming *of the Lord shall not prevent them which are asleep.*

1 Thes 5:23 *And the very God of peace sanctify you wholly; and I pray God your whole spirit and soul and body be preserved blameless unto the* coming *of our Lord Jesus Christ.*

2 Thes 2:1 *Now we beseech you, brethren, by the* coming *of our Lord Jesus Christ, and by our gathering together unto him.*

2 Thes 2:8 *And then shall that Wicked be revealed, whom the Lord shall consume with the Spirit of His mouth, and shall destroy with the brightness of His* coming.

2 Thes 2:9 *Even Him, whose* coming *is after the working of Satan with all power and signs and lying wonders.*

James 5:7 *Be patient therefore, brethren, unto the* coming *of the Lord. Behold, the husbandman waiteth for the precious fruit of the earth, and hath long patience for it, until he receive the early and latter rain.*

James 5:8 *Be ye also patient; stablish your hearts: for the* coming *of the Lord draweth nigh.*

2 Pet 1:16 *For we have not followed cunningly devised fables, when we made known unto you the power and* coming *of our Lord Jesus Christ, but were eyewitnesses of His majesty.*

2 Pet 3:4 *And saying, Where is the promise of His* coming? *For since the fathers fell asleep, all things continue as they were from the beginning of the creation.*

2 Pet 3:12 *Looking for and hasting unto the* coming *of the day of God, wherein the heavens being on fire shall be dissolved, and the elements shall melt with fervent heat?*

I John 2:28 *And now, little children, abide in Him; that, when He shall appear, we may have confidence, and not be ashamed before Him at His* coming.

Appendix IV

A Study of the Word *Rapture*

The Greek New Testament occurrences of the Greek word *harpazo* as they are translated into the English equivalents (KJV). English equivalents are in roman type.

Matt 11: 12 *From the days of John the Baptist until now the kingdom of heaven suffereth violence, and the violent* take *it by* force.

Matt 13:19 *When any one heareth the word of the kingdom, and understandeth it not, then cometh the wicked one, and* catcheth away *that which was sown in his heart. This is he which received seed by the way side.*

John 6:15 *When Jesus therefore perceived that they would come and* take *him by* force, *to make him a king, He departed again into a mountain himself alone.*

John 10:12 *But he that is an hireling, and not the shepherd, whose own the sheep are not, seeth the wolf coming, and leaveth the sheep, and fleeth: and the wolf* catcheth *them, and scattereth the sheep.*

John 10:28 *And I give unto them eternal life; and they shall never perish, neither shall any man* pluck *them out of my hand.*

John 10:29 *My Father, which gave them me, is greater than all; and no man is able to* pluck *them out of my Father's hand.*

Acts 8:39 *And when they were come up out of the water, the Spirit of the Lord* caught away *Philip, that the eunuch saw him no more: and he went on his way rejoicing.*

Acts 23:10 *And when there arose a great dissension, the chief captain, fearing lest Paul should have been pulled in pieces of them, commanded the soldiers to go down, and to* take *him by* force *from among them, and to bring him into the castle.*

2 Cor 12:2 *I knew a man in Christ above fourteen years ago, (whether in the body, cannot tell; or whether out of the body, I cannot tell: God knoweth); such an one* caught up *to the third heaven.*

2 Cor 12:4 *How that he was* caught up *into paradise, and heard unspeakable words, which it is not lawful for a man to utter.*

1 Thes 4:17 *Then we which are alive and remain shall be* caught up *together with them in the clouds, to meet the Lord in the air: and so shall we ever be with the Lord.*

Rev 12:5 *And she brought forth the Manchild, who was to rule all nations with a rod of iron: and her child was* caught up *unto God, and to his throne.*